A Summer at Camp Floridian

Nancy B. Miller

Summary: Insight into life at a coed summer camp through the eyes of Susan Grant, a first year counselor. It's also a how-to guide, in fictional form, on solving the most common problems of campers.

Printed by BookBaby in the United States of America.
First Printing, 2019
BookBaby
7905 N. Crescent Blvd.
Pennsauken, NJ 08110•877-961-6878
info@bookbaby.com

The author can be reached by filling out the contact page at
www.NanMillerTimes.com.

I dedicate this book to Earl L Miller who has been my soulmate, partner, and husband for almost fifty years. He has truly honored our wedding vows and has always been my best friend.

ACKNOWLEDGMENTS

Many people played a part in helping to produce this book via their support and editing.

I wish first to thank my late parents, Becky and Bill Baren, who enabled me to attend summer camp for five years as a preteen and teen. After the book was initially written in 1964, my mother served as my first editor.

Sometimes there are unexpected benefits to 50-year high school reunions. I had lost contact for forty years with childhood friend, Renee Greene. I learned when we reconnected that Renee had been a reader for several publishing houses. She not only voluntarily helped with queries and a synopsis but did a complete edit of the book.

Tom and Elaine Reed, long-time friends, whom I had initially met through Midwest Travel Writers Association, have been the grammar and spell checkers for my travel web site NanMillerTimes.com for three years. Elaine voluntarily proofread this manuscript.

Finally, I wish to thank my wonderful husband, Earl Miller, who has been not only a constant supporter of all of my writing but also my partner on my web site. He is also my computer guru and willingly handled the formatting of this manuscript so it could be sent to be published.

Contents

PREFACE

Being a shy youngster, Nancy Baren Miller's parents sent her to camp for five years to make friends with children her own age. Two of those years were at Camp Universe near Wildwood, Florida. It's now a home subdivision. The other was at Camp Ocala in Ocala National Forest which operated from 1954 to 1979. It became a 4H camp for the University of Florida from 1983 to 2015.

After visiting friends at the Fort Lauderdale boarding school, which she attended during the first semester of her junior year, she caught mononucleosis. For the final thirteen weeks of that year, Nancy homeschooled herself in Coral Gables. She was not allowed to attend her high school classes.

In January, Nancy telephoned Camp Ocala to see if she could participate in its staff assistant program. This meant no pay but she wouldn't have to pay room and board either. They said "yes." The plan was put on hold by the camp owners when Nancy became sick. After flying through her final exams, Nancy called Camp Ocala. The camp owners again said "yes", but they added a provision. Nancy had to pay room and board besides working for free.

Her parents encouraged her to go. However, she declined, believing that the camp was being unfair. The day after the phone call, she set up her typewriter on the bridge table, gathered sheets of paper, and said, "If I'm not going to camp, I will start my own."

She based it on memories of the two Florida camps. For example, in the chapters on the talent show and *South Pacific*, the character of Janie has experiences similar to Nancy's. After eight weeks, *A Summer at Camp Floridian* was ready to be edited.

Her mother, a former newspaper reporter for the Portland Press Herald in Portland, Maine, worked with Nancy on editing. When it was finished, it was sent to Lippincott. The family thought Lippincott had lost it when they didn't hear from the publisher for ten weeks. Instead, the manuscript had successfully passed their first reader before being turned down. If their second reader had approved, Nancy would have been a published author at age seventeen. Her mother often said she wished they had sent it out to other publishers.

After college, Nancy had a job as a first year counselor at Camp Mountain Lake in Hendersonville, North Carolina. It is now also a home development. Upon her return home, chapter one became chapter two. A new chapter about Susan Grant's counselor training started the book.

Following graduation in 1969 from the University of South Florida, Nancy wanted to do activities that involved people so she walked away from writing. The book stayed in the closet until her mother was dying of cancer in 1987. She knew how much it had meant to her mother so Nancy retrieved the manuscript, edited it once more, and sent it out twice without success.

Nancy turned the next year to creating children's stories followed by a column for an Ohio weekly newspaper on RVs and camping. Her career grew as she turned to travel and RV writing for many newspapers and magazines. By the time she retired as a freelance writer in 2007, she had published more than 500 articles in over 30 sources, many of them national. She was a member of Midwest Travel Writers Association and Outdoor Writers of America from which she won writing awards. She also received recognition for her writing from the Ohio House of Representatives.

In 2012, 32 friends encouraged Nancy and her husband, Earl, to send them travel articles and photos during their motorhome trips. This turned into starting NanMillerTimes.com in 2014. The web site has become successful with readership throughout the United States and two Canadian provinces. It has more than 160 articles and 3,500 photographs. Focus is on attractions and restaurants found in small and midsized towns. It has received coverage in *Motorhome* magazine and Akron, Ohio's *West Side Leader*.

Since numerous readers have asked Nancy when she was going to write a book, she decided to rewrite, reedit, and publish *A Summer at Camp Floridian*.

Chapter One

Susan Becomes
a Counselor

On a warm April day in 1964, sprawled on a living room couch, Susan Grant carefully scanned want ads in the *Sun*'s classified section. Then she spotted it.

> CAMP COUNSELORS
> For Private Camp
> General, Riflery, Nature
> Swimming, Riding, Tennis
> Phone 555-0199

"Mom," she called out excitedly, "here's a camp searching for counselors. I'd love to do that type of work. I know I have the experience to handle children."

Her mother gazed up from the sweater she was knitting. "Are you sure this is how you want to spend your summer? It's the first time you'd be a counselor. You haven't been a camper for four years. Camps might be different."

"Maybe they have changed some, but I know kids haven't. I think I'll call. Besides, what other job can I get working in the sun with children?" She reached for a phone and dialed.

"Good afternoon Camp Floridian. May I help you?" came a voice from the other end of the line.

"Hello, my name is Susan Grant. I'm a sophomore at the University of Miami and was a camper for five years. I saw your *Sun* ad. I'm interested in a counseling position."

"Miss Grant, we are interviewing counselors this afternoon. Would you like to make an appointment?"

"Please."

"All right. Can you arrive in an hour? Let's say 4:00? We're in the Jefferson Building. Will we see you then?"

Susan agreed. She hung up, excited and hopeful, and immediately strode upstairs. She quickly dressed in her kelly green suit complementing her long chestnut hair that attractively swung over her shoulders. She stared at her reflection in the mirror. It revealed an image of a girl of medium height with dark brown eyes, a slightly turned up freckled nose, and a casual smile. She definitely looked her age - nineteen.

After one more look, she raced downstairs, dashed into her car, and drove to the Jefferson Building. On the fifth floor, she searched for room 541 and opened the door.

The receptionist glanced up from her paperwork.

"Hi, I'm Susan Grant. I have a 4:00 appointment." The clock's hands read 3:45. "I know I'm early."

"Won't you be seated? I'll tell Mrs. Warren, our camp owner, you're here. She just ended an interview. I'll see if she can meet with you as soon as you finish filling out this application." She handed Susan a sheet of paper with questions on both sides.

"Thank you." Susan glanced around the room. She spotted action photos of campers at swimming and archery and one of a sailboat on a lake. Her eyes also fell on a coffee table where a pile of Camp Floridian brochures lay. She reached over for one and started reading it as soon as she had completed her application.

The receptionist telephoned into another office. After she hung up, she announced, "Mrs. Warren will see you now." She rose and ushered Susan into a pine office which had more camp photos on its walls.

"Hello, Susan, won't you have a seat. I'm Mrs. Warren," the woman behind a large oak desk said. Mrs. Warren, a grey haired, short and plump lady, appeared motherly yet very businesslike.

"Thank you," responded Susan, settling into a lemon-colored armchair opposite the camp owner.

"I understand you're here in response to our ad. Am I correct?"

"Yes, I am. I'm interested in a general counseling position at a summer camp. I've been a camper for five years."

Mrs. Warren reviewed Susan's application as she sat back in her overstuffed easy chair. "You have been on intramural teams in high school. In what sports did you participate?"

"I've played softball and volleyball. I've also avidly followed several sports on television so I know the rules."

"Do you think you could teach them?"

"I could assist with teaching. I could also help with the waterfront as I participated actively in water sports when I camped. I don't want to handle one activity all day long."

"That's fine. Tell me about the next item on your application. It says you can produce a newspaper since you have done creative writing."

"I served as editor for three years at camp. I feel confident I can produce one as a counselor. Do you have a paper?"

"Yes, we do," Mrs. Warren nodded. "A very fine one. We find newspapers serve as excellent souvenirs." She paused and glanced down at the application, then at Susan, before adding, "Susan, I definitely agree you could be very helpful with our camp activities. In particular, both your sports and paper experiences could prove beneficial. Tell me, why do you want to be a counselor? You wrote on your application that you love children and would rather work with them than do anything else. Why?"

Susan paused and then responded, "Because I have two younger brothers, we had a lot of children around our house. I've become interested in working with youngsters. Counseling would be a good experience."

"That sounds fine. Now let me describe our camp to you. I think our slides might interest you."

As Mrs. Warren projected a series of slides, she described camp procedures and layout. She turned to Susan. "Susan, we have an opening for a general counselor in Bunk 6, the ten-year-olds. Would you be interested?"

"Definitely. I'm impressed by your description of Camp Floridian and by the slides you showed me. That would also be a perfect age group for me to work with."

"Fine. I'll make out a contract now. Take it home, think about it, and mail it back. Please return it as soon as possible since we have had a good response to our ad."

"I sure will."

Mrs. Warren typed out a contract and closed the interview. Susan drove home, excited and contented. Even if she only received $300 plus room and board for the eight weeks, she would gain experience. Besides, she would spend the summer the way she preferred--as a camp counselor. She wondered what her ten-year-olds would be like.

Several weeks passed after Susan sent in her contract. One morning, she received some camp literature. It consisted of a brochure, a booklet of camp regulations for her to study, a recommended clothing list, and a medical form to be filled out by her doctor.

She carefully read the material and went to her physician within the next week. In addition, Susan constantly sewed on name tags and bought the necessary clothing. Excited about the camping season, she could barely wait until June 20--the first day at camp for a week of counselor orientation. Finally, time to leave home had arrived.

Following a seven-hour train trip, she found herself briefly alone at the Leesburg train depot. A young man soon approached her, wearing a pair of navy shorts and a Camp Floridian sweatshirt.

"Hi, I'm Jerry Martin. I live with Bunk 4 boys. You must be Susan," he greeted her. "Let me take your suitcase."

"Yes, I'm Susan. Thanks for picking me up."

"Mrs. Warren told me you were arriving at 3:00 so I decided to be of service. Besides, it is much easier to pick up girls than to paint equipment. Much more up my alley, anyway," he grinned.

"Well, thanks. You said your name is Jerry?"

"Right." He lifted her suitcase and teased, "What do you have in here? Rocks?"

They walked together toward a car which had in large letters on its side, "Camp Floridian for Boys and Girls." He put her suitcase in the trunk, opened the door for Susan, and they started the nineteen-mile trip back to camp.

After they had driven several miles, Susan inquired, "Have many counselors arrived?"

"No, but everyone should arrive later today or tomorrow. What will you teach at camp?"

"I'm Bunk 6's general counselor. Have you been here before, Jerry?"

"I worked here last year. This will be my second year on the waterfront. I love the water."

"I like fishing and boating myself. I used to go to the beach quite often at home last summer," commented Susan.

"I see we have something in common. Where do you go to school? I'm a second year med student at the University of Miami."

"I'm a sophomore at Miami," replied Susan. "You don't look old enough to be in medical school," she added, after looking at his boyish features, sandy blond hair, big blue eyes, and tan muscular physique.

"I'm ancient, really. I'm twenty-three."

Soon they approached Camp Floridian. A sign on a weathered fence post informed them that they were about a mile from camp. Susan suddenly turned to Jerry, "How good a camp is Camp Floridian?"

"A typical private camp. Mrs. Warren tries hard and has excellent facilities and activities. I think you'll like it here."

Susan eagerly looked for Camp Floridian's buildings. She spotted a grouping of light yellow, concrete structures. This was her home for the next nine weeks.

As soon as Jerry parked his car, she thanked him for the ride, retrieved her suitcase, and dragged it to a cabin marked "Bunk 6." The room was desolate except for four green metal bunk beds with mattresses standing on a green concrete slab floor. A wall of shelves, which looked like little boxes which opened in the front, piled one upon another, lined the cabin's rear. At the building's front was a small green patio which Camp Floridian had described in its brochure as a front porch. Each cabin also had its own green bathroom with a lavatory and two wash basins, in addition to a small shower stall.

"Green seems to be a big color here," decided Susan. "It reminds me of all the grass around here."

She leisurely unpacked her suitcase and put her clothes in the wall of shelves better known as cubby holes. Then Susan sat on the edge of a bottom bunk reflecting on her decision. Camp Floridian wasn't at all rustic. It didn't meet with her ideas of what a camp should look like. Pictures she had seen were primarily of activities. Had she made a mistake? Would she be happy here?

One way existed for her to handle the situation. She would devote almost all her time to work. She would not be content until she had solved all her campers' problems.

Next she thought, "No, that won't work. I want to date also. I don't know what to do. Maybe I should have taken an office job instead."

She left the cabin and wandered over to the rec hall where trunks and duffle bags of campers and counselors had been delivered. She found several counselors already searching for their belongings, and she joined in to try and find hers. At last, she located her old Army trunk and had it hauled to her cabin. She would return later for her duffle bag which she had also spotted. Dinner was in an hour at the mess hall so she had to hurry and get settled; otherwise, it was too tempting to take the next train back to Miami.

At dinner, Susan learned the names of several of her fellow counselors. Mrs. Warren had given out plastic name tags to be worn at all times to make it easier for counselors to get better acquainted. The mess hall seemed to come alive as conversations grew louder.

At the meal's end, Mrs. Warren stood up, asked for attention, and addressed the group. "I'm glad to see all of you here. I know, with a little effort and understanding on your part, we will have a wonderful summer. Since some counselors won't be at camp until tomorrow, we won't have our first meeting until 2:00 tomorrow afternoon. In the morning, I want all of you to make sure maintenance delivers your campers' trunks and duffle bags to your cabins. I also want you to assist in setting up equipment, taking an inventory of supplies, and submitting to me a list of everything you think we ought to get. Tonight, we'll have a dance at the rec hall. If you have any record albums, please bring them with you. Do you have any questions about camp you would like to ask?"

One of the girls raised her hand.

"Yes, Kim?" Mrs. Warren responded.

"When will we be able to see all the camp facilities? Will we have a tour?" Kim asked.

"No formal tours around here. Remember. You're roughing it. I will show new counselors around camp tomorrow at 11:00. If you have no more questions, you're dismissed to finish unpacking and dress for tonight. See you at 8:00 in the rec hall."

That night, Jerry came over to Susan. "How about a dance?"

"Fine, Jerry." She strolled with him across the floor. They danced for a while.

"I've noticed you've been very quiet tonight. Anything bothering you?" he asked.

"No. Should there be? I had a long train trip today and I'm tired."

After sitting together for some time, Susan asked, "I'm curious. Who's the counselor, with the glasses, reading over there?"

"Mike Wilson, our drama counselor. I heard he's producing *South Pacific* this summer."

"I'd like to get to meet him. He looks interesting," Susan commented.

"He is. Come on. I'll introduce you." They walked over to Mike. "Mike, this is Susan; Susan, Mike."

"Hello, Susan," Mike peered up from his reading. "You're new here. Aren't you?"

Susan nodded. "What are you reading?"

"Oh, this book. I'm checking out ideas on producing children's theater. I guess Jerry told you that I'm the drama man around here."

"Yes, he did. I'm quite interested in that type of work. I produced, well, actually I became camper assistant of plays for several years. If you need any help, I'd like to give you a hand."

"Susan," Jerry interrupted, "would you like some bug juice? In layman's language, that's diluted punch."

"Sure, thanks, Jerry."

After Jerry returned with drinks, they sat and talked about theater and camp plays for another hour. Then she excused herself and returned to the cabin. It was a beautiful evening as a breeze rustled through the leaves, and the moon shone brightly across the lake. Camp had started to look promising.

Susan awoke the next morning not knowing, for a moment, where she was. She suddenly remembered breakfast took place in fifteen minutes and hurried to get dressed. While walking to the mess hall, she became pensive. Later today, Mrs. Warren would be assigning counselors to travel Sunday with campers from Miami. Susan hoped she would be picked. Meanwhile she'd be hearing lectures on rules and procedures and about the psychology of children. She couldn't believe how much she needed to learn.

After a staff meeting later that morning, and since Susan had the afternoon free, she approached the camp owner as she left the lodge. "Mrs. Warren, would it be all right for me to do some typing and office work? I've heard you need someone in that department."

"That would be fine, Susan. I'm headed to my office now. We need someone to type a list of our campers and counselors by cabins and to sort out the campers' keys into separate cabin envelopes. Come with me. You can start right now."

The two climbed a hill to the owner's office where Susan worked the remainder of the afternoon. Ted, the boy's director, and Pauline, who taught girls' general athletics, assisted. Both were physical education teachers who had been at Camp Floridian for several years.

Dinner and folk dancing ended the evening with Susan eagerly returning to her office work the next morning. She seemed to be slightly withdrawn. Mrs. Warren began to be bothered by Susan's attitude and called her aside that afternoon. "Susan, I've watched you the past two days. I'm concerned you don't want to mingle with other counselors. Tonight, I want you to attend the campfire and have a good time. Remember, a good camp counselor knows both work and fun are important."

"I'll remember to keep that in mind," Susan retorted.

"Fine. Now let's get to the staff meeting. We have some important details to discuss today. Please help me carry camper information files and keys to all the trunks to the lodge. I want to give them out."

When they reached the lodge, they found lively discussions among the counselors. Mrs. Warren raised her hand and called for attention. "On Saturday, I will need several counselors to return to Miami for a day in order to have our campers accompanied on the train Sunday morning. The following counselors will take a bus from here to Orlando then catch a flight to Miami. Please listen carefully to hear if I call your name."

Susan listened impatiently. At last, she heard her name. She was thrilled to be among those returning with campers.

After the meeting and dinner, a few counselors started a campfire and sat around it on the camp's bleachers. Jerry approached Susan. "Do you mind if I join you? Man, I'm beat. I just finished getting the waterfront in shape. That's some responsibility...painting the equipment shack, seeing skis and boats are in good order, and washing down the dock. Whew! I hope those kids appreciate it. I'm glad I have a general counselor and a junior counselor in my cabin this summer to take care of the boys while I'm busy being waterfront director."

Susan smiled. "I guess you must be exhausted. No wonder I haven't seen you much the last two days. I've been having it easy at the office."

"Actually, I planned to ask where you've been hiding out," joked Jerry. "How about taking a walk?"

"Let's go." Jerry put his arm around her waist. The two strolled to the beach. As they gazed across the water, they noticed the moon reflected in the lake. The lights of a resort on the other side glowed.

"Pretty, isn't it?" He reached down and kissed her on the forehead.

Susan tried to act as if nothing had happened. After a moment, she said to Jerry, "What's your attraction with water, Jerry?"

"I'm really part fish," he told her with a wink. "Susan, I want to know you better. I want to see you after you return with your campers."

"I'd like that, Jerry. I want to know more about you, too. By the way, why did you decide to return to Camp Floridian?"

Jerry paused as if to collect his thoughts. "I don't think I would return to a camp where children aren't treated with respect. Camp Floridian is different. Mrs. Warren seems more interested in helping children than in making money. She doesn't have to worry about the dollars since she is wealthy and runs Camp Floridian as a hobby. She once confided in me that it keeps her young."

"She's quite a woman," Susan agreed.

"I see it's getting late. I think we had better return to the campfire. I hear counselors will learn our famous camp songs tonight. Come on. Let's go." He took her hand.

As they reached the council campfire ring, singing was already in progress. Susan looked over toward Mrs. Warren. The camp owner saw her two counselors together and gave them a pleased smile.

"Jerry," contemplated Mrs. Warren, "would have a good effect on Susan. He would be just what she needed to prevent her from being overly conscientious."

Chapter Two

Train Trip to Leesburg

Susan, having rested during the night at home, had her parents drive her to the train Sunday morning. She remained very quiet as she anxiously awaited meeting her campers and silently reviewed information she had received on them earlier in the week.

"You're pleased with Camp Floridian, aren't you, Susan?" her father inquired while on their way to the station.

"So far, it's fine. I like Mrs. Warren, and the staff looks great. I just hope I can handle the responsibility of five campers. I'm a little worried."

"I don't think you should be, honey," her mother assured her. "From what you told us, it appears to be an excellent camp. All you need is some confidence. You'll do fine. Just remember how eager you were for this job when you went for your interview."

"I guess you're right, Mom. I'll just have to wait and see what happens."

"We would like to receive some mail from you occasionally, so please write when you get a chance," Mrs. Grant requested.

"Sure, Mother. Well, we're here. I'll see you in eight weeks. I'd better hurry and meet my campers." Susan kissed her parents, waved a quick goodbye as they drove away, and rushed into the station to where a Camp Floridian banner hung on the wall.

Some parents gave reminders to their children. Others wondered what a summer of peace and quiet away from their youngsters would be like. Excited and expectant children said "Hi's" to other campers and their final goodbyes to parents and friends who saw them off.

At the depot, campers had been sorted into age groups. They eagerly awaited the train to Leesburg, the stop nearest Camp Floridian. From there, they would pile into Camp Floridian's yellow school buses to take them the last nineteen miles of their long journey.

Aboard the train, Susan gathered those from her cabin together. "Hi, kids, I'm Susan Grant. I'm your counselor this summer. We're all in Bunk 6."

"Aw, we know your name. I'm Michele Reiner. Nobody calls me that. Hardly ever anyhow," announced a girl with pigtails.

"What do they call you?" inquired Susan.

"Micky," she responded, her green eyes staring at Susan. She was tall, had a pug nose, and freckles.

"I'm Lynn Kingston. I don't like camp." A voice came from the corner.

Susan looked over at her. The youngster did not seem ten but about twelve. Long, straight blonde hair descending down the child's back was her prominent feature. "Well, Lynn, we'll make sure you have fun anyway," Susan answered.

"Sure," sneered Lynn. "You do that." She gave Susan a look of disgust and returned to reading a teen magazine.

Susan paused for a second and thought, "I sure hope we don't have trouble with her."

"I'm Ann," piped up a youngster, tall and thin with short, cropped black hair with heavy bangs, and very dark brown eyes. A sketchbook lay on the seat next to her. She busied herself with watching scenery.

Susan walked over to a small youngster who appeared about eight-years old. "What's your name?" she asked, sitting beside the camper.

"Who me?" came a startled voice.

"Yes, you," Susan said pleasantly.

"Janie."

The child had medium length, brown hair; small features, and blue eyes. She was very tiny, very serious, and seemed very frightened.

Susan speculated that she hadn't been away from home before. "Janie, is this your first year at summer camp?" she asked.

"Yes."

"Wait until you see the horses and the lake. You'll have lots of fun. There's always so much to do at camp. I'll bet you'll have a great time," Susan said, smiling at her camper. "Why don't you join the others a few seats in back of you?"

She guided her over to where Micky sat. Perhaps, Micky could make Janie feel at ease. She remembered Micky was the only one of the five who had attended Camp Floridian before.

Also sitting by herself was a short, fairly heavy child. She slumped in her seat watching the others. The youngster had a straight nose, mousy brown hair, and wore glasses. She, like the others, dressed in the uniform of a white Camp Floridian T-shirt and navy blue shorts. She seemed very tense and uncomfortable.

"I'll bet you're Donna. Am I right?" Susan smiled.

"Uh huh, I'm Donna. You're our counselor?"

"I sure am," said Susan, sitting next to the child.

Donna returned to watching scenery while Susan mentally reviewed, for the second time that day, information in the camper files. She remembered Micky was the experienced camper as she had attended Camp Floridian last year. She had actively participated in all activities except those at the waterfront and resisted all efforts to get her to join in swimming classes. According to her mother, she was terrified of the water due to Micky, at age four, having seen a toddler, who almost wasn't saved, tumble into a pool. Her mother had written that this year Micky must overcome her fear of water and learn how to swim.

Susan thought Micky could be the one to make the others feel comfortable as well as answer questions about camp. Gazing at the child, she noticed how calm and composed Micky was and how she made an effort to make Janie feel at ease.

Ann stared at scenery and busily sketched in her sketchbook. Susan remembered Ann's mother was an artist and had specifically stated that Ann must be allowed plenty of time for her artwork.

"Well," observed Susan, "it seems she's taking her mother's advice seriously." She smiled and shook her head.

Janie appeared to reject Micky's friendliness. She pulled out a pack of comic books and started reading. Micky walked over to Susan.

"I tried to talk to her. I guess she wants to be quiet. Anyhow, she wants to read. Can I join you?"

"Take a seat," replied Susan.

"Why don't we start some games?" coaxed Micky. "That's what we did last year on the train. It made the trip go faster."

"That's a great idea. All right, girls, let's play some games. Any suggestions?"

"Buzz," said Micky.

"Fine. Janie, would you like to be the leader?" inquired Susan.

"No, I'm not interested. I want to read."

Susan nodded. "All right. Maybe you'll join us later."

She recruited campers from other cabin groups, appointed a leader, and started the game. The girls participated enthusiastically for about an hour. Soon it was lunch time.

"Girls, I'm giving each of you two sandwiches. Today we have bologna and cheese as well as peanut butter and jelly."

"I want a peanut butter and jelly." "Me, too." "Let me have a bologna sandwich." "Is that all you have?" were assorted replies to Susan's announcement.

"Everyone, quiet down. You get one of each," proclaimed Susan.

"Can we trade?" asked Micky.

"Sure." She handed out sandwiches, cartons of milk, apples, and potato chips. The campers eagerly munched away. Although the trip was tiresome, they were still hungry.

After everyone finished eating, Susan requested, "Please pick up your trash and put it in the box when I bring it around."

Most of the girls followed her order. However, Lynn carelessly dropped her sandwich wrapper on the floor.

"Lynn, please pick up your paper," Susan requested.

Lynn looked disgusted at her counselor. "Why should I? You're not my mother. You can't order me around."

"Because I asked you to. That's why. Pick it up and put it in the box. Now!"

"I thought you were supposed to have fun at camp. If I knew camp was this way, I would have stayed home."

"Lynn, you have to give camp a chance. Camp can be very enjoyable. However, having fun also depends on you. Do you intend to pick up that paper or not?" reprimanded Susan.

"Fine." Lynn looked hostilely at Susan then deposited the wrapper in the box. "Are you satisfied?"

"Thank you, Lynn." Susan continued to pick up trash from other campers before sitting next to Donna. Lynn, she thought, seemed angry and unwilling to cooperate with the others. During the games, she had been domineering and determined to get her own way. Susan tried to remember what Lynn's camper file said. She could only recall one comment from Lynn's parents: make sure Lynn enjoys her first year at camp.

Donna seemed withdrawn and unhappy. She hadn't been drawn into games the campers had played before lunch. Now, she stared at the window, her head resting in her hand. Donna was the only girl in Susan's group who had never been away from her parents before.

Susan wondered whether Donna would be homesick. This wasn't unusual with this age group. She could remember when she had been homesick the first time she attended camp. The first night, after failing to understand why her parents had sent her away by herself, she had cried herself to sleep. Being age eight at the time, no amount of comforting by her counselor turned the tide of Susan's loneliness. She had learned it was necessary to get into the swing of things before she could enjoy camp life and stop being homesick.

"Donna, what's wrong?" asked Susan.

"Nothing. I'm fine," the camper mumbled, turning away from Susan.

"Are you sure?" Susan continued, very concerned.

"I'm fine," Donna insisted. "I'm a little tired. Do we have much further to travel? It seems as if we've been on this train forever."

"I know. Unfortunately, we have two more hours to go before we get on buses," Susan yawned, after glancing at her watch.

"I like to fly much better. It's quicker," commented Ann.

"You're right. Donna, why don't you see if Janie will let you read some of her comic books?"

"I think I'll read my own. Thanks, Susan." Donna reached into a package and brought out about ten comic books.

"You do have a collection," Susan agreed.

She sat back and relaxed. Donna was right. This trip was exhausting. She couldn't wait to get to camp and help her campers get settled. She wondered, "Will I make a good counselor?" She was worried. "Oh stop this," she told herself sharply. "You're not here to worry. You know you'll do just fine."

"Hey, Susan, look. Look at the orange groves and the hills. Wow! They're lovely," called out Ann excitedly.

"Yes, they are. I think Central Florida is the most beautiful part of the state. May I see your sketches, Ann?"

"Sure. I only did a few quickies. They're not great," Ann returned.

"Since you like art, I know you'll like arts and crafts. I think it's an activity almost everyone enjoys."

Ann perked up. "Will we have painting in arts and crafts?" she asked.

"What kind of painting?" inquired Susan.

"Watercolors, oils, acrylics. You know, real painting."

"I'm not sure," Susan admitted, after thinking for a moment.

Ann looked intently at her counselor. "I wish I could paint. I mean, do a good watercolor of orange groves," she sighed, turning to gaze at rolling hills covered with citrus trees. "I want to be an artist," she murmured.

"Really. That's very interesting. I want to be a nurse," announced Micky.

"Aw, you don't want to be a dumb nurse. I hate the sight of blood. Yuck!" insisted Lynn.

"Oh grow up," snapped Micky. "After all, if blood makes you sick, you don't have to tell everybody."

"Why don't you grow up, jerk?" retaliated Lynn.

Having heard enough, Susan intervened. After all, it wasn't smart to allow hard feelings to develop the first day. "Girls, let's play another game. How about, well, does anyone have any suggestions?"

"I do. Let's play Categories," shouted Donna.

"I want to be the leader," demanded Lynn.

"Let me, Susan, please," pressed Micky.

"Janie, wouldn't you like to be the leader? Come join us," pleaded Susan, still trying to get Janie into group activities. Janie had kept to herself throughout the entire trip.

"I don't want to. I'm going to sleep," answered Janie.

"Fine. Have a good nap. Donna, why don't you lead?"

"O.K.," Donna agreed. She started, "categories, names of trees, maples."

Her bunkmates and children from other cabins joined in, and Susan played with them.

They participated for over an hour when suddenly Micky called out, "Susan, we're coming into Leesburg. Look. There are the camp buses. Oh boy, I can hardly wait to see Sprinter. He's my favorite horse."

She was right. The train slowed as it entered the Leesburg station. On the platform stood Mrs. Warren and some counselors who had remained behind at camp. The campers became excited and started standing up.

"Girls and boys, please sit down until the train stops," commanded Susan. She walked over to some campers who had disregarded her instructions. "I said to sit down. Now go on."

"You're standing," one pointed out dryly.

"I don't care what I'm doing. SIT DOWN." Susan returned to her own group. "We should be at camp in about a half hour once we get on the buses." She pointed to two yellow school buses with "Camp Floridian for Boys and Girls" lettered on their sides.

"I'm glad we're near camp. I'm getting tired," complained Ann.

"I am, too," chimed in Micky. "I'm glad to be back. I love Camp Floridian."

Chapter Three

Arriving at Camp Floridian

After gathering all their belongings, campers and counselors disembarked from the train. With pushing and shoving here and there, they noisily boarded the buses. Having too many campers to go in one load, they sent the youngest ones ahead while Mrs. Warren called to send the two camp trucks.

As the buses rolled along the highway, most campers quietly watched the scenery fly past. Others read or carried on conversations. All anticipated their arrival.

"What does camp look like?" asked Ann suddenly.

"You'll see. It's lovely," murmured Susan.

"Come on, please tell us," begged Donna.

"You'll find lots of cabins and fields. The buildings are yellow stucco and very modern. We have a rec hall, mess hall, nature hut, and arts and crafts building. How about that, Ann?"

"You mean a whole building for art? That sounds great. I hope I get to work with the supplies I want."

"We'll see what we can do," answered Susan. "Micky, you've been here before. Why don't you tell the girls about it?"

"Well, it's super."

"Aw, it's probably some rinky dink camp. I don't know why my parents sent me here anyway," argued Lynn.

"No, it's not a lousy camp. I like it. You will too if you let yourself, Lynn," assured Micky.

"We'll see," Lynn sneered.

"Anyhow," continued Micky, "they have horses. If you learn to ride, you get to go on the trail. That's lots of fun. The cabins are nice, too. Can we decorate ours, Susan? I brought some posters."

"Sure. I don't see why not."

Micky suddenly yelled, "Hey, there's the Camp Floridian sign. We're about a mile from camp." She pointed to the same sign on the grey, weathered fence post Susan had passed a week ago. "Susan, can we go see Sprinter today, please?"

"We'll go on an exploration trip after you get your trunks unpacked. When we get to the cabin, girls, I want you to put all your clothes away. Please, first check everything for a name tag before you put it into your cubby holes. Everyone understand?" Her girls nodded. "I've already labeled the shelves assigned to you with your names. If you need additional room, please ask me."

It seemed like an eternity. The concrete buildings of Camp Floridian finally came into view. At last, campers saw what would be their home for the next eight weeks.

Some campers started singing "We're Here Because We're Here" while others began shouting. Peace and quiet became bedlam.

The official opening of the camp season arrived as the buses pulled up to the mess hall's front. Campers piled out in what appeared to be less than five minutes amidst shoving and shouts of "Hurry up." Counselors quickly corralled their campers and herded them toward their cabins.

Shouts of "I want to see the lake" and "Let's go see the horses" filled the air. These were soon hushed when counselors explained to their campers they would see the lake, horses, and the rest of camp as soon as they made their beds and unpacked.

Susan guided her group into their cabin. "Welcome home, girls."

"Home, hah. No television or swimming pool," griped Lynn. "You call this dump home?"

"No, but you'll find a beautiful lake for swimming that you'll see in a little while. Do you like horses, Lynn?" Susan asked.

"They have horses? I thought Micky was kidding. I can really ride?" Lynn seemed to brighten up.

"At last," pondered Susan, "I think I know how to get through to her."

"Sure. There are horses. Ten of them," she answered.

"I think I'll like it here," announced Ann, after briefly looking around. "This cabin isn't bad. At least it has a bathroom."

"Girls, here are keys to your trunks. Don't forget to check for those name tags," reminded Susan.

"Do you mind? We're not babies," pointed out Lynn.

Susan distributed the keys and helped with Donna's trunk. Her trunk lock had jammed, but with some effort, it opened. The girls sorted out their belongings and started to put their clothes away.

"No, Lynn, arrange your clothing in neat piles. Remember. We have to keep our cabin tidy." Lynn had thrown her possessions into her cubby holes instead of piling them in stacks. Susan walked over to help her. "Micky, you know how to put your shirts and pants into cubby holes. See if you can help the others."

At last, trunks were emptied and everything put away. Susan called them to her bed. "You will now learn how to make your beds a certain way. From now on, you are to tuck in your sheets with hospital corners."

She showed them the correct procedure. Her girls tried to copy her movements but were a little clumsy. Janie and Donna seemed disappointed that they had trouble making their beds.

"Never mind," soothed Susan. "we'll work on it tomorrow during cleanup."

"This place sounds like the army," grumbled Lynn.

"Yeah," agreed Donna. "Our maid always makes my bed at home. I never have to clean up."

"By the end of summer, you'll all be excellent at this," Susan added. "Besides, girls, inspections and cleanup aren't too bad."

"You mean we get inspected," protested Lynn. "What next?"

Susan decided to end this line of discussion. "How about a tour of the camp, girls?"

"Now you're talking. Come on, everyone," called Micky as she raced out of the cabin.

The others quickly followed. The girls almost ran to the arts and crafts building.

"Oh, Susan, wow!" exclaimed Ann, after she had glanced around the facility. "Gosh, they have so many machines here. I can't wait to get my hands on some of this equipment. This is great. When is our first arts and crafts period?"

"I knew you would like it. I'm not sure, Ann. I think we have arts and crafts tomorrow. I'll check it later this evening."

"Can we make things for our parents?" asked Donna.

"I'm sure you can," nodded Susan.

"We got to make ashtrays last year," announced Micky. "My mother was really pleased."

"I hope they don't have us draw. That's so babyish," commented Lynn.

"It's not babyish if you work at it," insisted Ann.

"I think you would all like to see the lake. Let's go. I'll show you where you can go swimming and boating. Do you like to swim?" Susan asked as they ambled downhill toward the water.

"I don't," admitted Micky. "I didn't go in last year. I don't like water, and I'm not going to learn how to swim."

Susan looked over at her and confidently assured herself, "That's what you think, Micky. We'll turn you into a water bug yet."

She asked the group, "How about the rest of you girls?"

"I can even water-ski," announced Lynn.

"That's wonderful, Lynn. I like to ski too. Can anyone else ski?" Susan inquired.

They shook their heads. "I can't even swim," muttered Ann. "Not well anyhow." The others nodded in agreement.

"Don't worry. I'll bet you'll all be fish by summer's end," Susan encouraged them, pointing to the lake. "Well, here it is."

"Susan, what's on the other side of the lake?" asked Ann.

"That's a resort," she responded, eyeing Donna and Janie. They had been quiet as if engrossed in their own thoughts and dreams. This bothered Susan. She told herself she might be imagining it.

"Do you like to play basketball and softball?" Susan asked as they headed for the playing fields.

"They're O.K.," shrugged Lynn.

As the girls strolled past the athletic fields on their way to the stables, Micky explained, "We had sports at least three times a week last year. We had volleyball, softball, basketball, and soccer. This year they're adding tennis for our age group. That's because they only teach tennis to those from ten years of age up. I played catcher on the softball team. That was lots of fun."

"Do we have to play when it's hot?" muttered Donna.

"Sometimes," replied Micky.

"Wait until you see the horses. Let's hurry Susan. I want to see Sprinter." Micky ran ahead.

"Micky, wait," Susan shouted.

They hurried and caught up with Micky. "Have any of you besides Micky ever gone riding before?"

"I have. I've had private riding lessons for two years," piped up Lynn.

"That's great, Lynn. How about the rest of you?"

Donna and Janie shook their heads. "I haven't, but I want to learn," announced Ann.

"They're good teachers here. You'll learn fast. Aw, please hurry, Susan." Micky grew impatient.

They finally arrived at the horseback riding rings, located a half mile walk from their cabin. Micky dashed to the stables. "Come here, Sprinter." A beautiful black horse responded to her call.

"He knows me. Neat!" said a delighted Micky.

"Wow! He's beautiful," agreed Lynn. "I want to ride him, too."

"He was my horse last year. I'm riding him. Get yourself another horse," argued Micky.

Lynn snapped back, "Look, Micky, just because you know so much about this camp, don't think you're telling me what to do. Don't think you're so smart either. I've been listening to you spout off. I'm sick of it. I'm going to the cabin." She started off by herself.

"Lynn, wait for the others." Susan hurried and caught up with her. "Lynn, please stay with us. Come on back."

Lynn angrily trudged back. She seemed irritated by Micky's assumed leadership. Would they compete for "head man" of the cabin?

Susan decided there wouldn't be conflicts if she could avoid them. After all, these children were here to have fun, not problems. She would not allow them to make issues of small matters.

"Come on, girls," she called as her campers petted the horses. "We've got to get back or we'll be late for dinner." After this warning, they started back.

The Bunk 6 girls reached the cabin where they changed from camp uniforms into fresh outfits before sauntering over to the mess hall for their first camp meal...a fried chicken dinner.

The entire camp stood while they said grace then scrambled into their seats. Susan served her group, who dove greedily into their dinners except for Donna, who picked at her food.

"What's wrong, Donna? Aren't you hungry? The food is very good. Why don't you try it?" encouraged Susan.

"I'm not hungry. Can I be excused? I want to go back to the cabin," blurted out Donna, pushing her plate aside.

"No," spoke up Susan, "You'll have to wait until everyone is finished. I think you'll like dessert. It's supposed to be chocolate pudding."

"Big deal," Donna mumbled.

"What's the matter? I'll bet you're homesick," jeered Lynn.

"Maybe she is and maybe she isn't," said Micky. "That's none of your business. Why don't you keep quiet? Anyhow, she hasn't been away from home before like the rest of us. I know. I asked her. I'll bet you were homesick the first time you were away from your parents."

"Now, girls, quiet down," reprimanded Susan. "Do you want seconds?" She noticed an increasing part of natural leadership on Micky's part. Lynn was self-centered while Micky was trying to mother her bunkmates.

"This is too much," Susan told herself.

During the remainder of the meal, the girls talked about different areas of camp they had seen. Donna withdrew even more. She seemed far off in her thoughts and had tears in her eyes.

They finally finished dinner and left the mess hall. Donna wandered back to her cabin with Susan and Ann. The other three visited Bunks 5 and 7 to get acquainted with others their own age.

Before they reached their cabin, Ann cried out, "Susan, look at the sunset. Isn't that a beautiful shade of orange? Look how the red and blue meet way over there."

"Yes, it's lovely. You'll see beautiful sunsets here, Ann," breathed Susan softly.

"All sunsets are the same to me. Come on," pouted Donna, impatiently.

"But they're not. They are all a work of art. I'm painting one this summer," insisted Ann.

"Who cares?" replied Donna.

"Are you feeling all right, Donna?" asked Susan, looking at her camper closely. She thought to herself, "Either she is sick, tired, or homesick."

"Ann, I have an idea. Why don't you join the others? If you hurry, you can catch up with them."

"All right, Susan." Ann headed after Micky's group.

"Come on, Donna. Why don't you tell me what's wrong?"

"I'm O.K. honest," Donna shrugged. "It's just that..."

Donna suddenly started racing toward the cabin. Susan scrambled to catch up with her. She found Donna standing beside her bunk, sobbing pitifully. She took her into her arms and sat with her on a lower bunk bed.

"What's wrong, Donna?"

"I want to go home. I want to be with my parents," Donna managed to evoke between sobs.

"You'll have a lot of fun this summer. I'll bet you'll love riding Skokie, the little grey pony, swimming, and hiking."

"I want to go home. I want to watch television. I hate it here." Donna shook hysterically, unable to say anymore.

"Donna, come on. Stop crying." Susan held her close and wondered what to do.

"Donna, let's talk. It might help."

Donna quieted as her sobs grew into quiet tears. She turned to Susan, "I'm sorry. Honest. I guess you think I'm a baby."

"Of course not. The first time I was a camper, I was homesick too. I hated it the first night and wanted to go home. My counselors tried to tell me homesickness was normal, but I wouldn't believe them. I thought I was a special case. It took me about a week before I enjoyed camp. You see, it was because I had to enter into activities first. Donna, it's natural to be homesick. Girls and boys of all ages suffer from it the first time they leave home. You're not a baby at all." She gave the child a tender hug. "I think I hear the others."

The other campers of Bunk 6 burst through the doorway. "Hey, there are a number of great kids in Bunks 5 and 7," announced Micky. She noticed Donna had been crying and gave Susan an understanding look.

Lynn also noticed Donna's tears and was about to say something. She stopped with an open mouth when Micky and Susan glared at her.

"I'm glad you're back, girls," started Susan. "Now change into jeans because tonight will be special. They've planned a campfire. You'll learn some of Camp Floridian's songs."

The girls changed into jeans and T-shirts. Susan prodded Donna gently, and they hurried outside as the whistle for line-up blew. The entire girls' camp strolled together to the campfire site, located near the counselors' lodge.

Tonight Camp Floridian held one of the season's special events. Campers sang old standards before learning the "Friendship Song" and "Alma Mater." This was their opportunity to meet other youngsters in their division whom they had not known before. Camp Floridian had two age divisions: the six through ten-year-olds comprised the juniors while the eleven through fifteen-year-olds were seniors. Sixteen-year-olds became counselors-in-training (CITs) while seventeen-year-olds were staff assistants, one step below junior counselor. The divisions sat together, making it easier for boys and girls to meet others of the same age. The entire camp attended the campfire.

Mrs. Warren opened the program. "Boys and girls, I'm so glad to see you all. I'm pleased so many old faces are back with our camp family this year. I'm also happy to see our new Camp Floridian campers and counselors. I hope all of you have a wonderful summer, learn new skills, and make many new friends. I'm sure the staff we've hired this year will make it easy to accomplish these goals. I want you all to meet our arts and crafts counselor, Jean Meadows. Jean, will you please come forward. She'll lead our singing tonight."

Jean held up a hand to quiet the disturbance among the older campers. "Let's start on one I'm sure you all know, 'I've Been Working on the Railroad.' Come on, everybody, let's see how loud you can sing."

After the camp had sung several other old standards, Jean called out, "We'll learn the 'Alma Mata' now. It goes like this:

"Shining lake, grassy hills
Oh dear camp with sky so blue,
All our life we'll remember
And give each day our love to you.
With the friends that we've made here
Sitting round the campfire light,
Those fond memories ever more
We'll think of each day and night.
Crafts and skills, we have learned
To help our lives grow strong.
To honor thee, Camp Floridian,
We raise our voice in song."

"All right, gang, let's try it. I want to hear you all attempt to sing it."

She started singing with the whole group joining. The new campers struggled to remember the lyrics. The "Friendship Song" followed the "Alma Mata." Sitting around the campfire, it was time to think or sing softly.

Mrs. Warren rose and addressed campers and counselors. "Thank you, Jean. Let's give her a Camp Floridian show of appreciation."

"Two, four, six, eight. Who do we appreciate? Yeah, Jean," the boys and girls shouted.

Mrs. Warren raised her hand to get attention. "Now we'll pass out popsicles. Please put your sticks and paper in the box nearby," she reminded them.

The campers pushed forward to get their popsicles, crowding others out of the way. While eating their treats, they mingled with other campers.

"Hi," called out a familiar voice.

Susan turned around and saw Jerry. "Hi, yourself. How's everything?"

"So far, fine. My boys are the rough and hardy types. How are your girls?"

"I don't know yet. One of my campers got homesick tonight after dinner. I think she's fine now. Your group is what bunk number, Jerry?"

"Bunk 4 boys, the nine-year-olds. I'd like to see you later tonight since I haven't seen you for two whole days. However, Camp Floridian has a sticky rule. All counselors have to stay in their cabins the first night. So that grounds that idea."

He thought for a moment. "What about in two nights? I have OD (Counselor on duty at night) tomorrow, but if you don't have OD, would you like to do something? There must be a pizza parlor close by. Come to think of it, I know just the place. How about it?"

"Sure. I can get off."

"Great. How do you feel about being a counselor now?"

"I don't know. I'll tell you in about a week. Right now, I'm kind of confused."

"Look," Jerry offered, "if you have any problems, I'm available. I have a very strong shoulder and I'm waterproof. Is it a deal?"

"It's a deal. Thanks, Jerry. I think we'd better get back to our troops now. Some of the others are ready to leave."

"Right," agreed Jerry. "See you tomorrow, Susan."

They rounded up their groups to take them back to the cabins. As they walked, Micky commented, "I don't think it's fair to make us leave now. It's still early."

"That's right," complained Lynn. "I don't believe this place. I get to stay up and watch television at home."

"This isn't home, Lynn," Susan reminded her.

"You're not kidding."

"I wanted to sing some more," protested Janie.

"Me too," agreed Donna.

"Girls, you'll appreciate an early bedtime around here. Tomorrow is a very busy day. You'll need as much rest as you can get. I want you to go straight to sleep when we reach the cabin."

The girls reached the Bunk 6 door, went inside, and continued grumbling while getting ready for bed. "I won't try and reason with them," Susan mused. "They'll learn tomorrow why they need a lot of rest."

When all the campers were in bed, Susan again addressed them. "Activities start tomorrow, girls, right after breakfast. I'm glad to have all of you in my group. I know we will have a wonderful summer."

She shut off the light and went outside to sit on the porch. "Am I glad?" she asked herself. "It looks like there may be problems. Each is such a distinct personality that there may be conflicts. However, if any problems arise, I'll solve them. I know I can."

She reflected on this for a few minutes and then turned her attention elsewhere. It looked like a wonderful summer ahead with maybe a little romance on the side. Jerry had made a hit with her, and she would enjoy helping her kids.

Her campers had fallen asleep. She was tired also and decided to go to bed. It had been a full day and an exhausting one. All was silent except for the chirping of the crickets. She could see an occasional flash from a lightning bug.

In a few moments, the majestic shadows of tall oak trees fell through the cabin windows upon the floor, unseen by sleeping campers and their counselor.

Chapter Four

First Full Day at Camp

The campers awoke to the blaring call of Reveille over the camp loudspeaker.

"Up, everyone," Susan commanded. "Rise and shine. Big day ahead."

Gradually, the campers sat up and dragged themselves out of bed. Reluctantly, they washed and dressed.

Within what seemed like too short a time, the whistle for line-up blew. Campers tumbled out of various cabins. After checking to see no one had been left behind, the counselors followed. Each cabin group's line looked like a bicycle spoke with the flag pole as the wheel's hub.

When every cabin was present, Jean had them announce, one by one, whether or not everyone in their group was there. All were except for one from a cabin housing the thirteen-year-olds. She, however, shortly joined her bunkmates.

"Why weren't you out on time? What is your name?" demanded Jean.

"Gosh, I had to put on mascara and eye shadow. Didn't I? Don't you want us to look cool? My name's Marilyn Coughlin."

"Marilyn, everyone has plenty of time to get ready. In fact, you have a full half hour. I insist on everyone being on time. I expect counselors to make sure all campers are at the flag pole before breakfast. If you don't have enough time, I'd advise you to rise a little earlier. Will two girls from your cabin please raise the flag?"

They hoisted the stars and stripes followed by the singing of the "Star Spangled Banner" and the saying of The Pledge of Allegiance. Jean read the announcements. They included the daily activity schedule for each cabin group and the news that trunks would be collected within the next two days.

She ended by saying, "Have a wonderful summer, girls. See you here tomorrow -- same time, same place."

After announcements, everyone went to the mess hall for breakfast. Although the campers were hungry, they groaned when Susan dished out plates of scrambled eggs and ham.

Donna grumbled, "Yeah, this reminds me of home."

"Come on, girls, eggs are good for you. Lots of protein. Besides, our camp cook makes delicious meals," coaxed Susan.

"Hey, Susan, these can't be eggs. They look like deflated rubber," pointed out Lynn.

"Lynn, stop right now. If you don't like the food, don't make any rude remarks about it as other people may care for it," scolded Susan sharply.

"Yeah, don't you have any manners?" added Micky.

"Aw, shut up," fumed Lynn.

"Quiet, both of you. I don't want to hear any more arguments for the rest of the meal." Susan noticed Janie was just nibbling at her food. The child had remained quiet except for an occasional "yes" or "no" and had kept to herself at the campfire last night. Susan gently asked, "Janie, what's wrong?"

"Nothing," Janie responded with a shrug.

"Susan, what time do we go to arts and crafts? Jean said we had a class today. I can hardly wait," broke in Ann enthusiastically.

"I'm not sure. I forgot to check it last night. I'll check when we get back to the cabin. I have a full listing of times for all of the week's activities. I see you're anxious to have arts and crafts," Susan grinned.

"Oh, yes," breathed Ann, her eyes sparkling.

Bunk 6 soon finished breakfast and grumbled about cleanup as they returned to their cabin. Each camper received a job including first and second sweeps, bathroom cleaner, porch cleaner, and cubby hole inspector. All made their beds and straightened their cubby holes. Cleanup took about thirty minutes. A daily inspection followed.

They heard a loud rap on the door. A cheery voice called from the doorway, "Hello, everyone. Ready for inspection?"

"Hi, Jean. I think my kids are ready. Come on in," invited Susan.

Jean checked the cabin quickly. Since this was the first day, she didn't expect the cabin to be completely clean with trunks lying here and there around the room. She took the time to show the girls how to make hospital corners, reminding them that their beds would be made that way for the remainder of the summer. Except for the beds, Jean made no comment on the cabin's appearance. The girls accepted this to mean they had done a good job considering it was their first inspection. Susan was proud of them. They headed to their first activity – archery.

The archery range was a short distance behind the girls' cabins. Marla Long was their instructor.

"Hello, girls. What bunk number is this?" Marla greeted them.

"We're Bunk 6," announced Micky and Lynn, simultaneously.

"Welcome, Bunk 6. My name is Marla. My job is teaching archery. Today, you will learn how to string and unstring bows. You won't shoot."

She pulled a paper out of her shirt pocket and read to them the sport's safety rules. Marla added, "No one is to retrieve their arrows until I blow my whistle. If someone is dumb enough to disobey that rule, I will dock her for a week from her favorite activity. I will also end shooting for that day. Understood? Archery can be dangerous if rules aren't followed. Arrows can kill if you don't know what you're doing. For you new campers, docking means you won't be allowed to participate in a certain activity. Do I make myself clear?"

During the first half of the fifty-minute period, Bunk 6 learned about the history of archery, and Marla demonstrated how to string and unstring bows. During the remaining time, they practiced this technique with Marla harshly correcting their every move. Since Janie had been more adept than the others, Marla singled her out at the period's end to demonstrate the skills they had learned.

"I don't want to do it," protested Janie. "Please don't make me."

"Nonsense. Now show us what you have learned. I'll only take 'yes' for an answer," insisted Marla.

Janie stepped forward and tried very hard to string her bow. However, she fumbled and became flustered. "See. I told you I didn't want to do it."

"Well," scolded Marla, "I thought one of you looked promising in this class. Guess I was wrong. The next time, we will practice these same techniques until you have all mastered them. I want this class to be fun. Most of all, I want it to be safe. Unless you know what you're doing when you handle a bow and arrow, it won't be. See you all next time."

Susan thought to herself, "What does she think this is, the army? These are ten-year-old children. Of course, archery should be safe, but she doesn't have to badger them. When I offered to help, she insisted she had been trained to teach archery. My job was to be a general counselor so she didn't need my help. What does she think a general counselor should do? I can ignore her reaction toward me, but she had better not get on my kids again."

She noticed Janie sniveling. "Come on, Janie, what's the matter? You did fine. So what if you weren't perfect. I couldn't do as well as you did when I was your age. By the end of the season, you'll be one of the best archers --- or is it Robin Hoods --- in camp." She put her arm around Janie.

The child wailed, "I don't like her. She's mean. I didn't want to do it. She made me. I hate archery."

Susan comforted her, and Janie stopped crying. Susan's opinion of Marla wasn't pleasant.

The girls returned to their cabin to change into their bathing suits. A half hour general swim for the entire camp followed their next period, swim instruction. Bunk 6 campers would remain at the lake after their second activity.

Usually, as Susan had learned in orientation, second period lasted for forty minutes. This gave campers and counselors time to get into their suits before general swim. Having swimming class before general swim was unusual. Upon reaching the beach, Susan was surprised to learn that Jerry was their instructor.

"Hi," he greeted them, "So this is Bunk 6. Hello, Susan."

"I didn't know you taught swimming, too," Susan smiled. "I thought you were the waterfront director."

"Just part of the job," he retorted. "O.K., girls, get into the water. Wade in up to your knees and sit or kneel down to get wet. The water is great. It's really warm. How many of you can swim? Dog paddling doesn't count."

Lynn was the only one to raise her hand.

"That's why I'm here -- to teach you to swim. Susan will help me. By the time you go home, you'll all be able to swim the English Channel. Everyone, stick your heads in the water. You don't have to open your eyes unless you want to."

"Hey," he shouted to Micky, who had dipped down holding her nose. "No nose holding. That's not for real swimmers."

By the period's end, the girls, except for Micky, stuck their heads under the water without any fuss. They also learned the proper method of kicking in the water with Jerry or Susan leading them around individually while holding their hands as the girls paddled their feet. Jerry had tested Lynn and found she was an intermediate swimmer. His assistant, Kathy, would work with Lynn separately when Bunk 6 came for swimming class. He learned names quickly and by the session's end, he knew everyone in the group. Susan was impressed by how he took charge and handled children.

Right before general swim, Jerry approached Susan. "Bad news," he groaned. "I found out I have OD tonight. How about taking a rain check on pizza until tomorrow night?"

"Tomorrow night it is," Susan agreed.

Jerry was the type of counselor she wanted to be: one with understanding and humor, besides having the ability to gain the respect of children. Susan decided that was the difference between the types of counselors Jerry and Marla represented. It was Susan's opinion that camp was a place where children should have fun and learn at the same time. Learning should be enjoyable, not a boring or an unpleasant task.

During general swim, Bunk 6 played water games except for Lynn who swam. Janie, at first, didn't want to participate in the games. When she saw how much fun the others had, and because of Susan's patient encouragement, she finally joined in. Janie's problem was probably shyness, Susan thought, and wondered how she could help her.

Micky led the games when the whistle blew to end the swim. Shouting and laughing, they all clambered out of the water and retrieved their towels hanging on racks. Susan patted herself dry and led the girls back to the cabin.

"That was fun, "Micky commented. "Learning to swim may not be as bad as I thought. Isn't Jerry great?"

"Yeah, I had a good time, too," smirked Lynn. "Too bad, you babies don't know how to swim. Maybe we ought to get you buoys you can strap on your back. Then you can swim with the rest of us. You don't want to miss all of the fun."

"We happen to be enjoying ourselves," declared Micky. A chorus of "Yeahs" followed.

"Just because you are an intermediate swimmer, big deal," snarled Donna.

"Gee. I was planning to help you learn how to swim. It doesn't pay to be nice," muttered Lynn.

"I don't think you know how," hissed Micky.

"Girls, enough. Stop it, both of you. This is a fine way to start the summer," scolded Susan. "O.K. here we are." She opened the door to the cabin.

"Now get dressed. I don't want to hear any more arguments, Micky and Lynn. Both of you should change your attitude. Lynn, because you know how to swim doesn't make you superior to the others. Micky, let your bunkmates fend for themselves."

The campers quietly changed into dry clothes. When the whistle for lunch blew, the girls silently wandered over to the mess hall. Susan did not want to sound severe. However, she had decided if she and these girls were to live together for eight weeks, she would have to gain their respect -- now. It was strange how different five girls could be: each with a distinct personality and problem.

Before lunch, as before every meal, the camp said grace. Each day a different cabin group led the prayer. Today, Bunk 10 boys had their turn. Afterwards, campers and counselors sat down noisily at their tables. A peaceful minute developed into loud conversations and playful heckling of campers and counselors. They ravenously consumed tuna fish sandwiches.

Bunk 6's campers, however, said very little despite Susan trying several times to stimulate a conversation. She felt she had impressed upon them that she would tolerate no nonsense involving making others or themselves miserable. At last, lunch was over. The girls returned to their cabins for rest hour.

"While you are resting on your beds, you need to write a letter home today. Afterwards, I think it might be a good idea to take a nap," Susan announced.

"Aw ... naps are for babies," her girls protested.

"Fine. Then read after you write your letters. You need to stay quiet for an hour."

In about fifteen minutes, not content to lie on her bed, Micky piped up, "Susan, can we play jacks?"

"Have you finished your letters?" Susan answered.

"I wrote a postcard," Micky replied. "Well, can we?"

"If you're finished with writing, I don't see why not. Sure, go ahead," nodded Susan.

The girls played for a while. Even though they had protested, some ended their game, returned to their beds, and fell asleep.

"Well," thought Susan, "I'll bet this is the most active day some of them have ever had."

Rest hour went quicker than they realized it would. They soon left for their next activity. Ann was delighted because, at last, they were headed for what would soon become her favorite class.

Bunk 6 found arts and crafts in a small, yellow building near the mess hall. The well-equipped studio contained all types of paints and art materials including watercolors, oils, and acrylics. It also had machinery to punch holes in paper, equipment for metal and leather work, a kiln, and all sorts of scraps. It was the best-equipped camp arts and crafts building in Florida, or so Mrs. Warren proudly proclaimed in her camp brochure.

Susan thought it strange for Jean to be the girls' camp director and the arts and crafts instructor. She asked her about it. Jean's reply was she was only the temporary director. Mitzi Stein, the counselor scheduled to be the girls' director, had telephoned Mrs. Warren before camp opened. She had explained she wouldn't be able to come during the season's first few days because of illness. Since Jean had been Camp Floridian's most experienced counselor and knew routines and regulations, she had been appointed temporary director of the girls' camp.

Bunk 6, having met Jean just that morning, remembered her name. They greeted her pleasantly with a "Hi, Jean."

"Hello, campers, I'm glad to see you again. How would you like to take a tour before we start the arts and crafts program? I want to show you all of our equipment so you'll have an idea of what you can make this summer." She guided them through the building and announced that they would spend the rest of the period drawing.

"Oh, thrills," grumbled Lynn.

"Will we use oils or watercolors for painting this summer?" questioned Ann.

"We have oils and watercolors. However, you must be eleven years old in order to use them. If you like to draw, we have poster paints as well as pastels and crayons for campers your age. Do you like to paint?"

"That's all she has been talking about," interrupted Lynn.

"My mother is an artist. She taught me how to paint when I was a little girl. I only used crayons at first. Now, I'm into acrylics," explained Ann, who then demanded, "When do we get to work?"

"First tell me your names. Then I'll start the class," answered Jean. The campers introduced themselves. Jean tried to match as many names to faces as possible.

"Susan, how about helping me pass out paper and pencils?" Jean asked, seeking aid from Bunk 6's counselor. This Susan did cheerfully, and the campers started to work.

The period moved faster than the others. Five minutes before the end of the class, Jean asked Bunk 6 to show what they had accomplished. While they had worked, she had offered encouragement and suggested ideas to girls who didn't know what to draw. The results were the type of artwork one would expect from ten-year-olds. Pictures of landscapes and flowers predominated. One was exceptional, however. Jean was surprised a ten-year-old could be so talented. Although Ann loved art, they didn't expect her to be so gifted. She showed a highly developed skill. The others in Bunk 6 stood with open mouths when they saw the sketch. Ann had begun a portrait of Donna which showed a marked resemblance.

"Wow, is that me?" gasped Donna. "Can I have it?"

"Sure," admitted Ann as she proudly handed it to Donna. "That's you. How did you guess?"

"Because it looks like me," came the reply.

Lynn and Micky became involved in a full-fledged argument as to whose picture was better. Susan soon settled this disagreement as she had stopped so many others since breakfast.

She now wondered, "What on earth can I do to keep these two from fighting? I don't want to dock them this early in the season, but they're always on each other's backs."

She took a deep breath, frowned, and told them once more, "Girls, you are treading on very thin ice. Stop fighting with each other. You're at camp to make friends, not enemies. You can't enjoy camp if you are always quarreling among yourselves. Now, I mean it, stop it once and for all."

During arts and crafts, Janie had been, as usual, quiet. Donna started to mope again. This meant more problems were in store for Susan. She was still wondering what to do about Janie's shyness. Janie knew the girls yet refused to speak unless spoken to; and then, only with one or two words. Susan remained concerned about Donna's homesickness.

At last, they left for their fourth activity: riding. They found the stables near the rifle range, reached by following a marked trail in the woods from the girls' cabins. At the stables, Red Dickens, the horseback riding counselor, met them. Red had on a checkered flannel shirt, straw hat, and jeans. His given name was Tom. All one had to do was to see his carrot-colored hair to understand why he received his nickname. Red had his own farm about three miles from camp where he raised horses. Thus, he had wide experience for such a responsible job.

"Well, hi, y'all," he drawled. "My name's Red, Red Dickens. I'll teach you to ride. I love horses and hate to see them mistreated. You will learn how to ride correctly as well as how to care for them. You'll find ten horses at this camp. Usually, two groups ride at the same time. Because of this, you may not get to ride at every session, and you won't have your own horse for the summer. However, they are all good horses. Some are as gentle as lambs and won't go beyond a trot while others will canter. I have some rules for y'all to follow. The first few times you come here, you won't go faster than walking the horses. We'll gradually go at a faster pace. If you want to, later on, you can trot. When I see anyone riding at more than a trot during these early stages, they won't ride for the rest of the day. I don't care whether you have ridden before or not. I hate to see people get hurt. Some of these horses get a little tough to handle at times. Today, we will learn about the horses. I think y'all saw them yesterday. Let's go look at them now."

He led them over to the riding ring where horses were tied to fence posts.

This was Susan's introduction to tall, lean Red Dickens. She liked the way he handled children, making them feel older. While giving them the responsibility of helping to care for and treat horses properly, he showed he would tolerate no nonsense.

Micky called out, "Dibs on Sprinter. That means he's my horse the first time we ride."

Lynn immediately became assertive. "No Dibs. I want to ride him, turkey."

They started word-fighting again, calling each other names while glaring steadily. Susan refused to tolerate this. It seemed as though they quarreled almost constantly.

Susan commanded loudly, "That's it. The next time I hear you two fighting, you'll both be docked from canteen for two days. No candy, no soda pop, no junk food of any kind. I mean it." She separated the girls, who continued glaring at each other.

Susan interrupted Red, who was giving a lecture about two different types of horses: Palominos and Arabians. "I told you to stop. If you keep this up, neither of you will ride Sprinter during the next riding session. Is that understood?"

Both girls looked at the ground after one more meaningful glance at each other. "Sorry, Red," Susan added.

"That's fine. Looks as if you have a couple of coyotes there. Now about Palominos," he continued.

The girls became bored and restless. They weren't interested in long lectures. They only wanted to ride. Some of the campers now perched themselves on top of the ring's fence rails; others walked around aimlessly.

Susan thought to herself, "At least, they will know something about horses when the summer is over."

After the class, while the campers cleaned up and prepared for dinner, Donna suddenly burst out crying again. Susan went over to her, "What's wrong, Donna?"

"I want to go home," wailed Donna. "The activities are nice, but I miss my parents."

Micky walked over to them. "I remember the first time I was away from home. I cried my eyes out. I hated it."

Donna continued weeping. "Micky, please," interrupted Susan. "Now, Donna, as I told you last night, after you get into activities, you'll have fun. You won't be homesick anymore. Why don't you participate in the camp play which Camp Floridian will have this summer? I'll bet that will be fun."

"Yeah! Everyone is homesick the first time away from home. We all miss our parents, but no one else is crying," pointed out Lynn. "I mean..."

"Lynn," scolded Susan. Donna was still crying when the whistle blew for dinner. Everyone was ready except Donna and Susan as they hadn't changed from jeans to shorts and fresh blouses.

"Girls, hurry and line up at the flagpole. Donna and I will be with you in five minutes." She gave Donna a hug. "Now go scrub your face. You'll feel better after dinner. Everything will turn out fine." Susan and Donna quickly washed and ran outdoors just in time to hear Bunk 6 reporting whether they were present.

"Susan, why weren't you with your group? You know counselors are to be at lineup," rebuked Jean.

"Sorry. We had a little problem in our cabin," admitted Susan.

"Is it all straightened out?" Jean asked.

"Yes. Everything is fine now."

Bunk 8 girls lowered the flag whirling about as the breeze from the lake reached it. Jean dismissed campers and counselors to go to the mess hall. By now, Donna had stopped crying.

The girls, stimulated by the day's activities, were starved. At the mess hall, between bites, they kept discussing the four activities. Even Janie seemed more talkative tonight. In between dinner and evening activity, they had time to themselves before leaving for the "sing" in the camp rec hall.

In addition to everyone participating in singing, the counselors presented a skit about camp life. Susan didn't participate, but Red, Jerry, and Marla did. It was amusing, especially to those familiar with camping. Susan's group still talked about it when they returned to their cabin. Since they were ten years old, Bunk 6 had the same bedtime as the younger children. Those eleven and older attended a nightly dance. All the Bunk 6 girls weren't pleased with this disadvantage and complained bitterly.

Janie appeared to be enthralled with the play. Susan wondered why. This was the first time Janie had shown any real interest in camp life. Susan wondered if it was because Janie would now know what to expect, or, perhaps, because she was interested in drama.

Bunk 6 undressed for bed, still chatting among themselves. Even Micky and Lynn agreed the counselors' play was enjoyable. As usual, however, they found some point upon which to disagree. This time it was which counselor was the best actor. Lynn thought it was Red while Micky gave her support to Jerry. For the first time since camp started, they did not argue but merely stated their opinions.

"Well," thought Susan, "at least they can discuss something peacefully. I guess I got through to them."

Taps sounded for the campers in Bunks 1 through 6. Susan said "good night" to her girls; comforted Donna, who was sniveling again; and praised Ann, once more, for her excellent work in arts and crafts. At last, after fifteen minutes of saying "good night," Susan left. She would not be sitting OD for three nights and decided to stroll to the lodge where counselors congregated after "lights out." The lodge was an old, white, wooden building, previously the farmhouse, before the property was turned into a camp. It had a large stone fireplace, overstuffed couches, and wooden rocking chairs. Mrs. Warren kept the pine tables replenished with magazines on children and camping.

A few counselors sat around the lodge. Others arrived after finally getting their campers to bed. Susan read until she saw Jean enter the building.

"Hi, Jean," she called out.

"Hi, yourself. Got your crew to bed already?" Jean greeted her.

"A long time ago. Do you have a minute? Can we talk?"

"Sure. What's on your mind?"

Susan explained she wanted Jean's opinion about campers and their problems. They sat in a quiet corner. Susan then asked, "Jean, what should I do? I have two campers who constantly have arguments. I've been to camp before but as a camper. I've never been a counselor."

"Susan, I can understand you might have a problem here and there since this is your first counseling job. The problem you mentioned is one of the toughest to handle. Do either of these children have leadership qualities?"

"Well, Lynn thinks she is superior because she had private riding and swimming lessons and can swim better than the rest. She's the only one who brought designer clothes and a stereo to camp. She's spoiled and argumentative."

"What about your other camper?"

" Micky, I think, enjoys playing the role of little mother, but she is overprotective. She seems to feel she has to do this because one is very quiet and shy while the other is homesick. Ann, thank goodness, seems well-adjusted but interested in one thing ... art."

Jean stared at Susan for a moment. "You need to impress on Micky how important it is to let each girl take care of herself. Remember, one important thing learned at camp is independence. If the girls lean on Micky all of the time, they won't learn to stand on their own two feet. Lynn needs to be reminded a good camper tries to help rather than antagonize her bunkmates."

"But why do they have to have so many arguments?" questioned Susan.

"They argue because neither is a leader. Both can be developed into one. Get your girls interested in activities. It's a sure cure for homesickness and helps to build confidence. Encourage Janie. Make sure she understands she is as good as anyone else. All will work out. I'm sure," Jean concluded.

"Thanks, Jean. I'll try your advice," agreed Susan.

They talked about camp routines and college. Susan glanced at her watch and realized it was time to retire. Although counselors could stay out until 11:30, she had undergone a full day and was tired. The two counselors said good night. Susan was surprised Jerry had not come to the lodge when she remembered he was one of the ODs.

Having reached her cabin, she paused and smiled. Although being a counselor sometimes presented problems, she still enjoyed her job. On this pleasant tone of thought, she opened the screen door of her cabin.

Chapter Five

Danger at the Waterfront

Days and weeks fly by when people are occupied. So it was at Camp Floridian as camp's second week came to a close. All problems in Bunk 6 continued including intermittent spats between Lynn and Micky.

Although Susan had tried to persuade Lynn to teach instead of boss, Lynn refused to respond to Susan's ideas. She considered herself superior to everyone in her group and refused to accept them as her equals. She continued to ridicule others harshly when they made mistakes. Lynn constantly reminded them their beds weren't neat enough for inspection. When they had trouble learning the crawl in swimming class, she made cutting remarks. Micky battled with her when Lynn assumed this "I know it all" attitude and continued to play the role of little mother of Bunk 6.

Twice, they reached the point where they almost came to blows. Although Susan didn't want to use punishment, she had to do so in these instances. How could she stop ten-year-olds from quarreling when they refused to listen to her? Neither reasoning nor punishment solved the problem. Docking proved useless. Finally, Susan decided she would have another talk with Jean.

Donna remained slightly homesick although nightly bouts of crying had long since ended. She had a role, as a chorus member, in the camp play, *South Pacific*, and actively engaged in camp activities.

Ann proceeded to enjoy arts and crafts. Jean had started a sketching class during optional periods in which Ann participated each day it was offered.

Optional periods had started during Camp Floridian's third day. In the morning, campers went to their activities as a group. In the afternoon, they went to a group activity followed by two individual activities they chose for the week. On Saturday, campers made their selections for the forthcoming week. Group activities consisted of nature, arts and crafts, horseback riding, tennis, swimming, campcraft (which included preparation for a night spent out-of-doors), boating, archery, and general athletics. In athletics, girls had softball, volleyball, soccer, and basketball while boys had baseball, football, basketball, and soccer. Optional activities offered were drama, sketching, typing, ceramics, fishing, golf, gymnastics, newspaper (which Susan taught), water-skiing, horseback riding, and extra swim instruction. Thus, campers would go swimming and riding with their cabin group and join extra classes if they wished.

Susan continued to see Jerry at the lodge after taps whenever they weren't on OD. They would go for walks, splurge on pizza, or just enjoy each other's company talking about camp. Marla was still a disciplinarian with the campers. She demanded perfection with each technique before proceeding to another in archery. She refused to let the girls shoot until they had mastered the fundamentals of aiming and loading the bow. Each time they shot their arrows and made a mistake, she corrected them harshly. At the end of four classes, however, they had become experts in some of the fundamentals.

Marla had Janie demonstrate time and time again, raising her voice when the child did not succeed in mastering the skill taught during each class. Janie had started to come out of her shell. She also had a part in the camp play. Mike Wilson, the drama instructor, had learned that Janie had taken a few drama lessons at home and persuaded her to become his assistant.

With today's optional activities over, Bunk 6 changed into jeans. After evening lineup, they hurried to the mess hall. The camp sat for dinner after saying the customary grace.

"Susan," grumbled Donna, "are we having movies again tonight? I don't like them. They're old, and all we've seen are westerns."

"We have movies and boating every Friday night, Donna. Don't you like sitting in the open air, watching the sunset, and feeling the breeze from the lake? It's really special," Susan answered.

"The reds and oranges are beautiful. I still want to paint a sunset," Ann insisted. "I wonder if Jean will help me with those particular colors in art class."

"You and your sunsets," snapped Lynn. "Do you think you're the only camper Jean has to work with?"

"I'm sure Jean will find time to help you, Ann. Just ask her. I think a sunset would make a lovely picture," commented Susan.

"Lynn, why don't you admit it? You're a little envious when someone can do something better than you," broke in Micky.

"Why should I be jealous?" Lynn countered, with a toss of her head. "After all, I'm glad someone in our cabin can do something better than I can. It does get a little boring knowing the rest of you can't do anything well."

"What do you mean, 'can't do anything well'? What makes you so superior?" With this outburst, the others turned their heads. They were surprised to see Janie take a stand. Micky usually took the position of defending the girls against Lynn.

"Well, Miss Robin Hood, I can't explain why I'm so much better. I guess it's natural," retaliated Lynn, brushing her long blond hair off her face.

"Aw shut up," Micky exploded.

"Girls. Please. This evening let's be different and try to get along with one another," Susan urged.

The girls grudgingly agreed and talked quietly for the rest of the meal. At last, they were excused, and Bunk 6 started toward their cabin. Donna suddenly turned to Susan. "Susan, I'm not homesick anymore."

"So I've noticed, Donna. Is it because you've been busy?"

"I don't know. I don't miss my parents as much anymore. Now I want to stay for the rest of the summer."

"I'm glad to hear you say that," replied Susan. "I know you are in the chorus. I wondered if you might be interested in participating in the camp talent show. You have a very nice voice."

The girls reached the cabin. Donna entered without saying a word. Susan was under the impression the child would jump at a chance to perform. She would ask Donna again about it at some later date. The talent show would not take place for another week.

Since this evening's activities included boating and movies, the campers could choose the one they preferred provided they had qualified in swimming. Everyone in Bunk 6 wanted to go boating. However, only Lynn was permitted to do so since the rest had not passed their beginners swimming test. It was a camp rule that a camper must first pass this test in order to go boating at night. Susan told the others they would not be able to go along.

"Well, it looks like I'm the only one to have fun tonight," Lynn announced, her voice dripping with sarcasm.

"I've seen that old movie anyhow. It's a drag." She would not let an opportunity pass to needle her bunkmates.

About 7:00 p.m., they all headed out to the pavilion by the lake. All but Susan and Lynn sat down on the grass with the girls from Cabin 5 as they waited for the movie to start.

Susan and Lynn continued to the rowboats. They rowed in the same boat with two girls from another cabin. The rowboats glided swiftly through the water toward the middle of the lake, where they would pause before heading back. Susan's boat lagged behind the others. In order to get to the middle, they had to pass through a large clump of overhanging trees located just beyond the camp boundary.

While beneath the trees, something suddenly fell into the boat. Lynn screamed and stood up; the rowboat overturned; and everyone landed in the water. As Lynn fell into the lake, she banged her leg against the boat with a sickening thud. Susan glanced around to make sure the other two girls hung onto the boat's side and were safe. Meanwhile, one of the other rowboats in the area hurried over. Mitzi was in that one.

"Susan, I'm headed to the docks to get Jerry. He'll pick you up in the motorboat. Don't attempt to turn the rowboat over. Just hang onto the bottom of it," Mitzi commanded.

"Right. I understand."

After this exchange, Mitzi and her rowboat crew started furiously back.

"Susan, help me," came a voice.

Susan looked around at Lynn. "What's wrong?"

"My leg. It hurts. I don't feel so good," Lynn sobbed.

"Wait a second. Hold on. I'll be right over to help you."

Susan swam over to Lynn. "Easy, easy, Lynn. Hold on. Jerry will be back for us soon," Susan said, hoping it would bring comfort. What was taking Jerry so long?

Lynn passed out and started sliding under the water. Susan grabbed her under the chin and held her head up. She looked around at the others and told them not to panic. One had screamed when Lynn blacked out.

"Girls, Jerry will be here soon. Hold on tight. You're both big girls. Screaming won't help," Susan said firmly.

The other rowboats remained a distance away. Only Mitzi's boat had been in the immediate area when the accident occurred. Marla's boat returned to check out what had happened to Mitzi's and Susan's boats.

"Marla, hurry," Susan cried out.

Marla continued rowing toward her. "What's wrong? Did you have an accident? Surely you ought to know how to handle a rowboat by now," she sneered.

"Look, I need help. Lynn is hurt. I'm not sure how badly. Please help me."

"Darling, it seems to me, you always need help. You're doing fine. Just continue to hang onto Lynn," answered Marla.

Susan was desperate. No other rowboats were close. "Forget about personal differences. Would you please help me? Take these other girls into your boat. I know it is dangerous for a boat to be overloaded. Please, take at least one, Marla."

"These are small boats. But I'll do you a favor and take them into my boat. Now you do me a favor. Stay away from Jerry."

"Fine. Anything. Girls, into Marla's boat. Careful you don't overturn it," ordered Susan.

Marla helped the girls into her rowboat. Susan was becoming exhausted. Why didn't Mitzi and Jerry hurry? She felt her grip slipping. As if in answer to her thoughts, she heard a motorboat.

"At last," Susan sighed.

Jerry and Mitzi appeared. After what seemed like an eternity to Susan, Jerry was beside her relieving her of Lynn. Susan then climbed into the boat, with the aid of Mitzi, and they started back. When they reached the shore, Jerry hopped out and carried Lynn to the infirmary. Alice Robins, camp nurse, immediately took charge of the situation. Susan followed the nurse into the examining room. Mitzi was already there.

"What's wrong with her?" Susan asked, her voice quivering.

"It looks like a snake bite. Also, there appears to be a very deep gash. It's bleeding badly."

"Snake bite? Oh, no!" exclaimed Susan.

"I doubt if any poisonous snakes are in this lake. However, we had better treat it that way. How long since it happened, Susan?" The nurse had already begun treatment.

"I guess it happened about twenty minutes ago."

"No, Susan," interrupted Mitzi, "It only seems that way. It has been ten minutes since you overturned. Alice, can I do anything?"

"Yes, call Doctor Thomas at once. Tell him what has happened and for him to let the hospital know to expect us. The number is on the wall next to the phone. I have finished what I can do. We need to get her to the hospital now. Tell Doctor Thomas to meet us there."

"Right," replied Mitzi, who immediately swung into action.

Although Susan was still a little foggy about everything, she started to come out of it. When the nurse repeated the words, "Possible poisonous snake bite," Susan became alert.

"Alice, what can I do? Please, she is one of my campers."

"Nothing now," assured the nurse.

Mitzi came into the room and reported, "Doctor Thomas said he will meet us at the hospital."

"Fine, Jerry, carry Lynn out to my car. Susan, you come with us. Mitzi, tell Mrs. Warren about the accident. Let's go," commanded Nurse Robins.

"Alice, what about the other girls in my cabin? Who will take care of them?" questioned Susan. She suddenly wondered who would stay with her girls after the movies since she would be with Lynn.

"Mrs. Warren will send a junior counselor or staff assistant to take care of them. Don't worry. Now come on, please, we're wasting time. Lynn is still semiconscious," the nurse explained.

Nurse Robins, Susan, and Jerry raced toward the hospital after they left the camp gates. Jerry drove. Susan turned to the back seat where the nurse had her camper stretched out. Nurse Robins was taking the child's pulse.

"How is she? Will she be all right?" questioned Susan in a faltering voice.

"I don't know how bad the bite is. This gash will require stitches. I think she'll be fine, but I don't like this shock she is in. Don't worry, Susan. Doctor Thomas is an excellent doctor," Nurse Robins replied.

Susan knew they were traveling fast. However, it seemed like hours had passed before they drove to the front of a hospital. She saw a stretcher and a doctor. "Were they waiting for Lynn?" she wondered.

Jerry barely came to a full stop before the attendants rolled the stretcher up to the rear car door. They lifted Lynn out and hurriedly pulled her into the emergency room. Nurse Robins had started talking to Doctor Thomas when Jerry and Susan entered.

"Her pulse is rapid. She has lost blood. She passed out and has been semiconscious for about a half hour. I'm not sure what kind of snake bite it is since I have had little experience treating this kind of bite. I treated it as if it was a poisonous snake bite, Doctor," Nurse Robins replied to the doctor's questions.

"Fine. Good job, Alice. I'll take over now. Who are these people?" he inquired.

"The girl is Susan Grant, the child's counselor. The boy is Jerry Martin."

Doctor Thomas examined Lynn. "We're in luck," he announced. "This isn't a poisonous snake bite. It looks like a harmless water snake bite to me."

"But why is she dazed?" sputtered Susan.

"Shock, Susan, from the loss of blood from the deep gash she has suffered. The bite didn't help matters either. I'm treating her for it now. We'll have to put in some stitches. I'm admitting her for observation for a day or two as a precaution."

"Will she be all right? How can you be certain it is a harmless bite instead of a water moccasin bite?" Susan pressed, the tension showing in her voice.

"Now, young lady, calm down. There is nothing to worry about. We can tell it is a harmless bite because the skin is only slightly red and swollen. A poisonous snake bite is much more inflamed," answered Doctor Thomas with authority.

Lynn stirred sluggishly. The doctor bent over her again. "I think she's coming out of it, Alice," he announced. "Come on, Susan, she'll be fine."

Lynn blinked, opened her eyes, and gazed at the examining table where she lay. She stared across the room. "Where am I?" she muttered drowsily.

"You're in a hospital room, Lynn. I'm Doctor Thomas. Now take it easy," the doctor assured her when Lynn tried to get up. "Lie back down. You have lost some blood and have had quite an experience for yourself. How do you feel?"

"Dizzy and my leg hurts. What happened?" Lynn looked puzzled.

"Some snake decided he liked raw Lynn so he decided to have some for a snack," declared Jerry.

Susan bent over Lynn and cradled her in her arms. "Oh, Lynn," she repeated over and over.

Nurse Robins gently pulled Susan away from the child and told her to wait outside in the hall. Jerry followed them into the corridor. The nurse returned to the examining room.

Susan looked as if she were about to burst into tears; perhaps from tiredness and tension, perhaps from relief. Why was not important.

"Susan, don't cry. You'll get waterlogged, and you have had enough water for one day," soothed Jerry in a low voice. He took her into his arms and held her closely.

Back in the examining room, Lynn asked weakly while trying to sit up, "When can I go back to camp, Doctor Thomas? What's wrong with Susan?"

"Susan is fine. Now lie back down. That's a good girl," prodded the doctor.

"I have to get back to camp," insisted Lynn. "I want to go riding tomorrow. Ow, my leg. Why does it hurt?"

"It's the gash that hurts. We have taken some stitches and want to watch you for a few days. That is why we're not allowing you to go back to camp tonight. I want to keep you here tomorrow. Just lie quietly. I'll get someone to take you to your room."

"Aw, please, Doc. It doesn't hurt too much." She winced. "Well, maybe it does."

"Alice, may I see you outside for a moment?" Doctor Thomas requested.

"Why of course, Doctor." They went outside, leaving Lynn with an emergency room nurse.

"I suggest when you get back to camp that you give Lynn's counselor a sedative. I am keeping the child here for observation overnight. I think she will be able to go back to camp either tomorrow or the next day. I'll call you," the doctor spoke quietly.

"Fine. I'm relieved everything is under control. This is the second snake bite I've ever handled."

"That's understandable. You did the right thing. Now I suggest you get Susan back to camp. She's had a bad experience tonight and appears to be under severe strain," Doctor Thomas suggested, "Good night." He strode back into the emergency room.

Nurse Robins walked over to Susan, sitting quietly with Jerry. She explained Lynn would be in the hospital at least one day and recommended they leave now. The two counselors rose. Susan kissed Lynn goodbye as an orderly wheeled the child to the ward. The three left the hospital with Susan feeling relieved that Lynn would receive proper care and be all right.

When they returned to camp, even though Susan assured her she was fine, Nurse Robins insisted Susan come into the infirmary for the night and gave her a sedative. Then the nurse went to report the latest facts to Mrs. Warren and informed her Susan would remain in sick bay overnight.

Mrs. Warren decided to call Lynn's parents after hearing the nurse's report. Despite the late hour, she telephoned and informed them of their daughter's mishap. The Kingstons immediately became agitated that such an accident had occurred and refused to be appeased. They insisted they would come to camp to see Lynn and refused to accept their daughter would be all right until after they had seen her for themselves.

At last, the telephone call was over. Mrs. Warren, disturbed over the night's happenings, thought, "Some parents are impossible. Yet, in this case, I can hardly blame them."

All was quiet. Susan could not sleep until she had been reassured by Nurse Robins that Lynn would be fine, and Tracie, one of the junior counselors, had taken over Bunk 6 for the night. As the sedative took effect, she drifted off in slumber.

The next morning, Susan returned to her girls who quickly gathered around her.

"Where is Lynn?" inquired Ann. "Is it true a snake bit her?"

"She's in the hospital. How did you girls know about the bite?"

"I asked Tracie where you were. She filled us in," admitted Donna. "We missed you."

"How did it happen?" asked Micky.

Susan sat and related the boating incident story. Little did she realize her tale would be repeated time and time again, spreading around camp like a wildfire. She started her campers off to activities and to what she hoped would be a period of normality.

Later that day, she received news from Nurse Robins. Lynn would leave the hospital that afternoon and was much better. She had not suffered any other complications. Lynn would have to remain in the camp infirmary for a few days. However, at least, she would be back from the hospital.

Lynn returned at five that afternoon. About 7:00 p.m., Mrs. Kingston arrived. She hurriedly walked from her car and inquired of the first counselor she met, "Where is my daughter? I have to see my daughter."

The counselor asked who she was and directed her to Susan's cabin.

"Hello, are you Mrs. Kingston? I'm Susan Grant, Lynn's counselor," Susan greeted her. "We've been expecting you."

"I want to see her," Lynn's mother demanded.

"She is in the infirmary, Mrs. Kingston. If you'll come with me, I'll take you there." She guided the distraught woman to the infirmary and turned her over to Nurse Robins.

"My baby, my baby," Mrs. Kingston greeted Lynn, wrapping her arms tightly around her.

"Hi, Mom. What are you doing here?" asked Lynn.

"Darling, when I heard what you had gone through. Such agony! All thanks to your irresponsible counselor. I couldn't leave for our European vacation. I want you to come home with us. Next time, I won't listen to your father. Camp is no place for you."

"Susan is not to blame, Mom. Besides, it's not too bad here."

"Then who is to blame? She was the only counselor in the boat. You're not to blame."

"Mom, of course, I'm not to blame. Maybe it is Susan's fault. She hasn't been the most fantastic counselor in the world. Besides, she's punished me by docking me twice this summer."

"Susan, you punished, Lynn? I'll have to talk to Mrs. Warren about you. You certainly have your nerve."

"Mrs. Kingston," addressed Nurse Robbins in a professional manner, "Susan Grant saved your child's life. She prevented your child from drowning. Lynn will be fine now. She has received excellent care from a trained medical doctor. I don't know how a snake bit your daughter, but I can assure you, Miss Grant had nothing to do with it."

"Well," huffed, Mrs. Kingston. "Well."

"Mom, I don't want to go home unless I can go to Europe with you and dad."

"I'll have to discuss that with your father. First, I want to speak with Mrs... what's her name ... Warren about your counselor. I don't see why camps can't hire competent help."

"I'm sorry that you feel I'm inadequate. When you speak to Mrs. Warren, I would like an opportunity to be there. I feel I know the full details of Lynn's accident," Susan insisted firmly.

"Very well. I believe in justice as much as I do not believe in camps for my daughter. She can't stand such rough living."

"Thank you," fumed Susan.

"I will see Mrs. Warren tonight after I take Lynn out to a restaurant for ice cream," announced Lynn's mother haughtily. "Get dressed, dear."

"I'm sorry, Mrs. Kingston, that is not a good idea. Lynn is staying right here. I have to follow the doctor's specific orders to keep her in the infirmary." Nurse Robins was adamant.

"How dare you. I know what's best for my daughter. Who do you think you are?"

"I'm a registered nurse, and I say Lynn doesn't go out." Nurse Robins brought Lynn back to bed. "I'm sorry, Mrs. Kingston, I know you want to take your daughter out for a good time. However, as I've told you, it may make her condition worse. Do you understand?"

"Well, I've never been so insulted in my entire life. You're right, you'll be sorry. Where can I find Mrs. Warren?"

After learning the location of Mrs. Warren's cabin, Mrs. Kingston went storming to the office and entered without knocking.

"Yes. Oh, hello, Mrs. Kingston. Won't you sit down," Mrs. Warren invited.

"No! Either you dismiss Lynn's counselor and your nurse immediately or I'll take Lynn out of this camp and give you plenty of trouble."

"I'm sorry you feel that way. What seems to be the problem?" Mrs. Warren asked softly.

"My daughter has been hurt due to the negligence of her counselor, Miss Grant, and what is more, I have been insulted by your nurse. What type of camp are you running?"

"We try to run an excellent camp. I'm sorry if we don't meet with your approval. I'll send for Miss Grant and Mrs. Robins, our nurse. I want you to hear their version of the accident. I require people accused of misconduct to be present. They have the right to hear what is said and be given a chance to defend themselves. Besides, I think they know the facts better than I could describe them to you. Is your husband here?"

"Mr. Kingston said he would be back at eight after I learned all the details. We had car trouble on the road, and he has gone to find a garage to fix it. Regarding your statement, I told your counselor I would not object to her being here. Your nurse can also be present when we discuss Lynn."

Mrs. Warren sent for Nurse Robins and Susan so they might hear the accusations against them. Mrs. Kingston continued her tirade and threats against the camp until a man strode in. He was bald, short, and potbellied and introduced himself as Mr. Kingston. Before his entrance, Susan and Nurse Robins had arrived and told their story amidst Mrs. Kingston's interruptions.

"I'm sure my wife has told you that we were worried about Lynn. That's why we came," he announced as he introduced himself.

"David, I want Lynn to come home with us. I feel her counselor has been negligent, and I don't want Lynn to suffer anymore," his wife complained. "Besides, Lynn said her counselor docked her. Docking sounds horrible. And, I see no reason why Lynn can't go out with us for ice cream."

"Wait a minute, dear," Mr. Kingston said. "I refuse to see anyone wrongly accused because we are upset. I'd like to hear Susan's story as well as the reason why Lynn isn't able to go with us. The whole incident may be no one's fault or Lynn's responsibility or the camp's laxity. However, it's unfair to everyone to act before we get all the facts."

Susan told her story again, being interrupted by Lynn's father as she went along. "Isn't it dangerous to boat under those trees? Has anyone ever been bitten before?"

The replies to his questions were negative. Nurse Robins explained Lynn should be kept quiet for a few days as she had received a shock to her system. Besides, she had just returned from the hospital that afternoon. The nurse carefully described the treatment Lynn had received. Nurse Robins also explained Lynn would be recovering in about three more days since she had received the proper care.

"My dear," Mr. Kingston said to his wife, "I don't see why we should take Lynn home with us. After all, her counselor saved her from drowning, and she received good care. What is docking, Susan, and why did you dock Lynn?"

"Mr. Kingston, docking is the taking away of a certain privilege such as attending camp movies or being kept from riding. It's only used when a child misbehaves and does something harmful to herself or others. I docked Lynn because she is constantly quarreling with another girl in her group. I docked both of them. It is not a serious punishment."

"I'm sure it is the other child's fault. My Lynn is such a good girl," interrupted Mrs. Kingston.

"Let her continue, Louise. I want the full story. Before we decide to do anything, we will talk to Lynn. I don't want anyone to be blamed unjustly."

"Don't you care about our daughter? How can you be so callous?" Mrs. Kingston cried.

He took her in his arms. "Of course, I care. However, I want more details as to why Susan punished Lynn."

"Well," Susan continued, "one girl uses her frustrations to insult the other girls while the other attempts to defend them. The two sometimes quarrel incessantly."

"I have a feeling that Lynn may be the bossy and sarcastic one, knowing her past behavior. Is she?" asked Mr. Kingston.

"I'm afraid she is."

"You needn't be afraid, young lady, because she acts that way at home. That's why we sent her to camp. I think Lynn has been spoiled by us. Everything material she asked for, we gave her. I had hoped she would make friends at camp. However, if she acts the same as she does at home, I doubt if she will. I presume the reason we gave her so many things and allowed her to become spoiled was because she didn't have many friends. If you help her to change her ways, I'll be very grateful. I'm sure my wife will too."

"David, camp may not be the solution for our baby."

"Why not? If she comes home, you know she will wind you around her finger again. I want our daughter to grow up. She is not a baby, Louise. She is almost eleven years old. She must learn how to get along with others."

His wife nodded in agreement with him. Mr. Kingston then asked to see their child, and they walked to the infirmary.

"Daddy," Lynn shouted when she saw him and tried to get off the bed.

Nurse Robins restrained her. "Lynn, stay in bed. You're not allowed up yet," she insisted.

Mr. Kingston approached Lynn. "What's this about your being bitten by a snake? Did you bite him back?" He gave her a hug.

"Oh, Daddy, am I coming home with you and mother? Please. I hate camp. My bunkmates don't know how to do anything, and Susan docks me."

"No, Lynn, you are staying for the remainder of the season. Do you hate camp because you can't always have things your own way?"

"Of course not," shrugged Lynn. "After all, why should I be concerned with getting my own way? I'm used to it by now. I mean, you and mom are leaving for Europe, and I have to stay at this crummy camp."

"Now, Lynn," her father interrupted.

Lynn continued, "Besides, I have a counselor who likes everyone better than me. So what can I expect?"

It shocked and puzzled Susan that one of her campers would say things like this. Why? In her opinion, she had been fair. Was it unfair to give equal treatment to all? Was that being partial in Lynn's opinion?

She listened carefully to Mr. Kingston and Lynn. She realized Mr. Kingston thought Lynn felt this way because she wasn't given special privileges and couldn't always get her own way. The child agreed this was true but wanted to come home anyway.

"Lynn, why do you think we sent you to camp? We wanted you to live with other children and learn how to make friends. Susan told me you constantly put down the others in your cabin. Why do you do that?"

"I don't know. How should I know?"

"Do you do it in order to feel superior or because you want to tease them?" he reprimanded her.

"David, stop it," commanded his wife. "I want to see you for a minute."

They stepped outside the infirmary. Mrs. Kingston moaned, "David, why are you talking to Lynn this way? Maybe Susan doesn't like Lynn and punishes her for no reason at all. Please don't be so harsh."

"I don't believe that for one minute, Louise. You know what Lynn is like at home. We sent her to camp for a reason-- to help her make friends or, at least, to learn how. Let's go inside. She's staying and that's that."

"I hope you know what you are doing," muttered Mrs. Kingston, as she followed her husband inside.

"Lynn, being a hostile person does not make anyone feel good inside, nor does it help you become a fine human being. It will keep you from making friends. Before long, you will be left alone by everyone."

Lynn started crying, and her father stopped talking and went over to comfort her. "Lynn, I know you don't want to hear you aren't coming with us. We want you to stop acting the way you have been behaving. It is not because we don't love you. We do very much. It is for your own sake that we want you to change. I want you to stop crying and listen carefully. If you start making friends because you show them you care, you'll have a wonderful summer."

"I'll try, Dad," sniffed Lynn.

"Honey, we have to say goodbye. We leave for Europe in four days and won't be back for Visitors Day," announced Mr. Kingston. He gave her a hug and kissed her on the forehead.

"I'll miss you, Mom and Dad. I wish you would come for Visitors Day, but I understand," said Lynn grudgingly.

Mrs. Kingston gave Lynn a long hug. "See you later, darling," she said as the Kingstons left.

"Susan," Mr. Kingston addressed her warmly as they walked toward the camp gates. "Thank you for saving Lynn's life." He motioned toward his wife, getting into their car in the camp parking lot. "I'm sorry Mrs. Kingston caused you so much trouble. She has babied Lynn, and Lynn has taken advantage of this since she was a small child. I guess her mother doesn't realize that Lynn is no longer a little girl. Well, thanks again."

"Goodbye, Mr. Kingston, have an enjoyable trip to Europe."

As Susan walked back to her cabin, she shook her head. "Thank goodness I'm off the hook. I'm glad Mr. Kingston understood. Maybe Lynn will stop being so impossible from now on."

Chapter Six

Marla is in Trouble

Sunday afternoon, Marla hesitantly walked down her cabin steps. She shared a cabin with a few other specialist counselors who did not have their own camper groups. Mrs. Warren had heard about her conduct in the boating incident and summoned her to the office.

As she slowly strolled, Marla thought to herself, "I'm in for it now. I knew I was wrong when I didn't help Susan immediately the other night. However, I was angry and couldn't help it. Sometimes I don't understand myself at all. I want this job. I want to stay here. It is so great to get paid for doing what I love. Besides, my being here makes up for all those years my friends attended camp, and I was too poor to go. I'm treated like a somebody here. At home, I'm just a nobody. I hope my story is believable enough to get me out of this jam. Aw, it will be. I'll make sure of it."

Having reached the camp owner's office, Marla rapped loudly on the door. Mrs. Warren looked up from the paperwork on her desk. "Marla, please come in."

"Thank you, Mrs. Warren. You wanted to see me?"

"Yes, I did. Won't you sit down."

Marla obeyed the request and sat in the comfortable old rocker opposite the owner's desk.

"Marla, has anything been bothering you lately? I have received a most regrettable report about you regarding the other night when the boating incident occurred. You were a very good counselor last year. That's why I asked you back. However, it seems, you have had your share of problems this year."

"I can't think of any problems. I'm enjoying being a member of your staff."

"Then I find no excuse for the other night. I have talked to other campers and counselors who were involved. I heard you would not take two of the campers immediately into your boat when Susan's overturned. I consider this a serious breach of trust and totally irresponsible on your part. If I did not know you any better, and had not been pleased with your work last year, I would have fired you by now. Before I make any decision as to whether or not you remain on my staff, I want to hear from you exactly what happened."

"What have you heard, Mrs. Warren?" Marla inquired.

"Just what I told you."

"That I hesitated about taking two of Susan's campers into my boat when hers overturned. Is that all?"

"Marla, isn't that enough? Susan had a problem keeping Lynn from drowning. You didn't want to cooperate."

"All right, Mrs. Warren," started Marla, "I'll explain my conduct."

"I'm waiting." The camp owner leaned toward her.

"Mrs. Warren, I thought about what I did. I realize it was extremely childish on my part. I didn't think."

"You didn't think. You didn't think about endangering campers' lives," Mrs. Warren exploded in disbelief. "I had confidence in you."

"Please," interrupted Marla, "let me explain further. I had three campers with me in my little rowboat. They barely hold five safely and that's pushing it. I didn't want to risk my boat turning over by overloading it. I thought having six people in my rowboat, or even five, would...well, I thought it would be too much."

"I also heard via the grapevine that when you finally took the girls in, you asked Susan to stay away from Jerry. Are you always so worried about yourself and your romantic affairs?"

"Not really. I was just concerned about the danger for the campers in my boat if I took those girls aboard. Oh, I like Jerry. But you must not believe I would... oh, I couldn't put myself above any campers."

"Marla, are you telling me the truth?"

"Of course," Marla lied.

"Sometimes, I don't think you know what the truth means. I'm beginning to be very sorry that I hired you. In fact, I think you had better make arrangements to leave tomorrow. I'll get someone else to handle archery for the rest of the summer."

"Please, Mrs. Warren." Marla was frightened. "I know I was wrong. Believe me, I know I should have handled the situation differently. Please let me stay. I promise I can handle my job from now on. Please don't fire me," she begged.

Mrs. Warren sat and stared at Marla, studying her counselor. "If I didn't know how well you handled your job last year, and that you're an excellent archery instructor, I would say definitely not. I know you have had a rough life and that you grew up without any advantages. But, Marla, as I said at one of our staff meetings, we try not to judge campers exclusively on their past environment at Camp Floridian. We take into account what kind of people they are now. I think this should apply to our counselors as well.

"I don't think a reprimand is sufficient in this case. I am willing to give you one more chance. I'll let you remain here at camp because most of your work has been satisfactory this summer. However, you can remain only if you agree to the following conditions. First, I want to see you every week, privately, here in my office for talks on how everything is proceeding. Secondly, stay away from the waterfront for the rest of the summer except on your days off. And, finally, if I hear about any other lack of responsibility on your part, you will be asked to leave immediately. Is that clear? I will not have any counselor endangering any camper's life."

"I understand. Thank you so much. I promise I won't cause any problems." Marla quickly left the office. She felt very tired and slightly discouraged.

The next morning at archery, Susan turned to Marla, "I heard something about you being called into Mrs. Warren's office."

"You heard right. I'll bet you're happy about that," Marla retorted.

"Maybe I should be, but I'm not. Oh, Marla, come on. Let's not be enemies any longer. Sure I like Jerry. I realize you do, also. Any girl who doesn't like a guy like him...well, I mean, he is easy to talk to and very attractive."

"Susan, you bore me." Marla turned. "Careful, girls," she shouted to Susan's campers. "Remember, keep those arms straight."

"You don't want to be friendly, do you?" snapped Susan.

"I only want to do my job. That is all I'm here for, not to make friends. Now, please go."

"Fine. I'll do that. I'll keep out of your way." Susan walked closer to her girls. She was amazed anyone could behave like that and wondered why Marla acted the way she did.

Chapter Seven

A Date with Jerry

That night, Susan's campers straggled back to the cabin as soon as evening activities ended. As on all Sunday nights, the distribution of popsicles and a brief "get together" session followed a campfire. The junior campers always went to bed at the end of the event while senior campers and CIT's assembled for a social at the mess hall.

As Susan's campers undressed for bed, Donna suddenly asked Susan, "Do you think Lynn will stop being so impossible to live with? After her accident, I don't see how she can continue to act that way."

"Heck, she'll probably think she's the best because a snake bit her," muttered Micky.

Susan interrupted, "Come on, girls, you should be nice to Lynn when she returns from the infirmary. Remember. Lynn doesn't have any friends here in camp. I'll bet she would like to be accepted by everyone."

"She doesn't act like it, so why should we be friends with her? A kid who wants friends doesn't always say 'I'm better than you' or 'Why do you do it so badly?'" responded Micky.

"Listen, everyone." Susan motioned for them to come to her. They gathered beside her bed. "Lynn doesn't know how to make friends."

"That's obvious. Maybe she's snake bitten," cracked Micky.

Ann broke in, "Micky, let's listen to Susan. Maybe we ought to show her how to make friends. After all, it isn't fun to be lonely all summer."

"Yes," Janie answered, "but how do we know she has changed? Besides, I don't think I want to be her friend after the way she has treated everyone in our cabin."

The others agreed, except for Ann, and Susan told them to think about it. She said good night to them and went to the lodge. Gratefully, she remembered she would not be on OD for the next two nights.

At the lodge, she saw Marla and Jerry sitting and talking together. Jerry stood and walked over to her as soon as she entered. Susan observed an instant change in Marla's facial expression from friendliness to hatred.

"Hi, Susan. How is Lynn?" Jerry greeted her.

"She's at the infirmary. Alice Robins wanted to keep her under observation for a few days. Did I interrupt anything between you and Marla?"

"We were just talking. She says you had trouble with the Kingstons."

"How did she know? I did have a problem with Mrs. Kingston, but her husband straightened it out."

"Hi, Marla," said Susan, approaching her.

"Hello." Marla immediately turned away and hustled out of the lodge.

"What's with her?" Susan asked Jerry, taken back by Marla's behavior.

"I don't know. I have a great idea though. As I told you before, I want to know you better. I know we see each other at swimming and here at the lodge for coffee and cake after taps. And it's true that we've gone out for pizza twice. Yet, we've still never talked about us. Instead, we've discussed camp and our bunk groups. I don't know much about you, Susan, and I'd like to. I'd like to very much."

"I noticed you have a day off tomorrow, so do I," he continued. "How about driving over to the Atlantic Ocean? I know of a wonderful restaurant that's a little over an hour from here. It's quiet there, overlooks the water, and has the best Southern fried chicken I've ever eaten."

"I don't know, Jerry," Susan paused. "It sounds great, but Lynn's still recovering. What if she needs me?"

"She has Alice to keep an eye on her. Didn't you say something about knowing each other better at the beginning of the camp season? If I remember correctly, it was the first night. Well, how about it?"

"All right, I'd like that," Susan admitted, as she smiled at him. To herself, she added, "He is persuasive." Susan was pleased. She liked this aggressive young man. In fact, she liked him very much.

They talked and decided to meet in front of the mess hall after cleanup. At about 11:00, Susan returned to her cabin with a sense of well-being, looking forward to her first all day date in three weeks.

The next morning arrived in a golden rapture of sunlight. Breakfast and lineup were uneventful. Before cleanup, Bunk 6 went to see Lynn. They stood outside her window at the infirmary. The girls had not wanted to go until Susan had gently prodded them. She was delighted with the group's decision to visit Lynn and to find the child feeling better.

"Hi, Lynn, how are you?" questioned Micky.

"I'm better. Thanks. I hope to be out of this place tomorrow." She paused and looked at them quizzically. Her bunkmates had strange expressions on their faces. "Did I say anything wrong?"

"You said 'thank you.' Was that a slip?" mumbled Janie.

Susan was distressed at Janie's remark. Perhaps, she surmised, Lynn might be taking her father's advice about trying to be pleasant and friendly. She needed to be encouraged, not discouraged, by Bunk 6.

"Aw scram. Go away," snapped Lynn. "Leave me alone." The rest of Bunk 6 wandered away, muttering that Lynn didn't act as though she wanted to make friends. Susan, they agreed, must be mistaken in thinking Lynn might want to change.

"Susan," Lynn called to her counselor, who was ambling away with the rest of the cabin group.

"Yes," she replied, turning back to Lynn.

"I do want to make friends. How can I if they don't let me?" The child, her eyes pleading, gazed intently at her counselor.

Susan was disturbed. She was even more certain that Lynn would change if the other girls would give her sufficient understanding. However, she doubted they could be convinced that Lynn would now make an effort to be friendly. She smiled and said soothingly, "Don't worry, Lynn. Just keep working at it."

Susan walked back to her cabin for cleanup and inspection. The girls worked at a snail's pace, or did it only seem that way because she was anxious to leave camp and keep her date with Jerry? Susan ordered her campers to "hurry up" in order to finish before Mitzi arrived.

Finally, Mitzi reached their cabin and completed her inspection of Bunk 6. Susan realized once Mitzi, the girls' director, arrived in camp, she was a person with experience and understanding. However, Susan still preferred to take her problems to Jean, who readily offered constructive criticism and encouragement.

With cleanup over, Susan became free to leave camp. After Tracie, the junior counselor, replaced her for the day, she left for the mess hall. Waiting for her in front of the building, she saw Jerry dressed in casual clothes and carrying a bundle.

"Hi, Susan. I'll bet I forgot to ask if you wanted to go swimming." He shook his head. "I'm sorry. Would you like to take a swimsuit? Next to the restaurant is a beautiful, white, sandy beach."

"No, thanks, Jerry. I don't think I'll go swimming this time. How about giving me a raincheck for counselor swim during rest hour tomorrow?"

"You're on," he answered. "Well, let's go. I've been waiting for this for weeks." They walked toward his car, a red karmann ghia convertible.

"I thought the Chevy you drove to the hospital was yours. This car is fantastic."

"Oh, that station wagon is Alice's. This one is mine. I bought it this spring."

Jerry helped Susan into his car then walked around to the other side. She leaned back against the soft, red, leather interior and sighed as she considered, "What a car!"

Jerry interrupted her pleasant thoughts, "Do you want to listen to the radio?"

"Perhaps a little later," Susan admitted.

"I know a place I think you'll love. It's peaceful and restful. We can talk there. As I said last night, I know so little about you. How about filling me in on the essentials?" By this time, they drove onto the country road leading from camp to the main road stretching far ahead.

They talked for a while, concentrating on their backgrounds and interests while admiring scenery as they drove. Jerry, Susan learned, wanted to be a pediatrician because he loved children. This was the main reason he took a job as a camp counselor. After they had traveled for about an hour, Susan decided the date was a wise decision since Jerry was fun and interesting.

"Jerry," Susan hesitated, not certain how to put her thoughts into words.

She wondered if a relationship existed between him and Marla. Susan believed in following the Golden Rule or at least a version of it, "Don't steal another girl's boyfriend and hope she doesn't steal yours." She wondered if Marla had any claims on Jerry. If she had, Susan would step aside and stop seeing him.

"Jerry," she continued, "is there anything between you and Marla?"

"Why?" he asked, raising his eyebrows and glancing at her.

"She has been cold toward me whenever she sees us together. For example, she was that way last night or when Lynn's accident occurred."

"Marla and I were friends for a couple of weeks at Camp Floridian last year, but we aren't anymore. I managed to see through her so-called phony charm after dating her twice. For some reason or other, I remained friendly with her. I didn't want to go out with any other girl counselors except Carol."

Susan interrupted him, "You don't have to tell me more."

Jerry drove the car onto the road's shoulder, let the motor idle, and looked over at her. "I've been wondering why you haven't been more eager to go out, Susan. I want you to know the truth about Marla and me. Last year at camp, Carol and I became friends. Marla told Carol lies about me. Carol believed them and that quickly ended any possible relationship."

"What did she say, Jerry?"

"Things she knew were untrue such as Marla and I were still dating; that I was a girl collector. Somehow or other, she still thinks I am 'her boy.' Don't let her nastiness bother you, and don't believe what she says about me."

He pulled onto the road and drove on, explaining they would be at their destination in about an hour. They drove in silence for about ten minutes. Susan thought about what Jerry had said. What was Marla trying to do?

"A penny for your thoughts," prodded Jerry.

"Oh, come on, they're worth at least a quarter. Inflation, you know. I was thinking about Marla. I don't like the way she badgers kids. If she is the type of person to cause trouble among counselors, why was she hired this summer?"

"Mrs. Warren believes campers should be under strict discipline when they participate in dangerous activities. Archery happens to be one of those. Marla is an excellent instructor and very knowledgeable about archery. That is why I became attracted to her. When the campers have completed her course, they may not be experts in hitting the bull's-eye; however, they have respect for the sport and know what they are doing."

Jerry paused for a moment. "You're a good counselor, Susan. Where did you get your experience?"

"This is my first year as a counselor. I was a camper for five years at camps in Florida and North Carolina."

"Where did you learn to handle your campers so well? I've seen many counselors. In fact, I've been one for three years. However, I've rarely seen a good first-year counselor, and you're one of them."

"Thanks. I have twin brothers who are now sixteen years old. They've given me plenty of experience in handling children. I just apply what I learned from dealing with them. Besides, I've been asking Jean for advice. She's really helped."

They talked a while longer before becoming silent. They listened to the radio and discovered they both liked the same kinds of music: jazz and easy listening. At last, Jerry parked his car in front of a weathered but charming, gray, wooden shingled shack. They strolled inside, and Susan realized Jerry had previously mentioned this restaurant. Jerry found a small table overlooking the ocean. The cozy restaurant had a rustic atmosphere.

"I hope you're hungry. The food here is marvelous," announced Jerry with a grin.

"I'm starved," Susan replied, smiling in return.

They both ordered what Jerry suggested -- the restaurant's specialty, fried chicken. They sat gazing out the window watching the Atlantic Ocean's waves lap the sandy white beach.

"It's beautiful, Jerry."

"I like it. It is a long drive from camp. However, it is one of my favorite places to eat. I lived in this area when I was a kid. I remember eating here time and time again. We moved away from here to the Gables when I was fourteen. But enough. Where do you want to go after lunch?"

"I'd like to go to that peaceful spot you mentioned. What is it, some sort of wayside park?"

"It's a museum," he revealed, "located about a half hour from here or would you rather go some other time?"

"No, I love museums. Have you ever gone to any of the famous ones in New York? They're fascinating," Susan insisted.

"I've never been to New York. I've heard their science museum is worth visiting. I'd like to go sometime."

The waiter served them their chicken and asked if they wanted their beverages refilled. He brought them two new Cokes. They finished their lunch and left for the museum.

"Jerry, you were right. That little restaurant has a great view and charm. The chicken tasted delicious. It was perfect," Susan commented as they drove.

"I'm glad you enjoyed it," he smiled.

Silence filled the car the remainder of the short ride to the museum. Throughout the building, Jerry explained, in detail, many of the technical and scientific exhibits. He amazed Susan with his knowledge. His inner excitement and the glow on his face when they looked at medical displays impressed her.

At about 5:00 p.m., they started back to camp after stopping for a quick dinner. On the way, they talked about all sorts of things: different careers, medical developments, campers, and camp. Jerry again complimented Susan on the methods she was using to handle her girls.

As they arrived at Camp Floridian's gate, Jerry looked over at Susan. "How about joining me next week on our day off?" he asked. "I've had a wonderful time."

Susan hesitated before saying, "It's been fantastic for me, too. Unfortunately, I think I'll probably have to stay in camp next Monday. I want to work on the talent show. Can I let you know later in the week?"

Jerry was not to be put off. "I'll check with you later. Remember too much time devoted to camp and not enough for your own recreation is foolhardy, Susan. Besides," he told her half joking and half serious, "I'm a demanding guy."

Jerry parked the car and leaned over. Their lips met as the two counselors warmly embraced. Then Jerry came around the convertible's side, opened the door, and helped Susan out of the car.

As she walked the hill to her cabin, Susan called back, "Thanks for a great day."

Dates with Jerry would be fun. She would continue to see him as often as possible at the lodge at night, during counselor swim, or rest hours. Yet, she wanted to work hard at her counseling job, even if necessary on a day off. She would have to think about which was more important...work or romance.

Chapter Eight

The Talent Show

Susan was tired but content when she returned to Bunk 6. It had been a full day and an exhausting one. She decided to lie down. Since her campers remained engaged in their evening activities, it was peaceful in the cabin. She soon fell asleep before shouting children abruptly awakened her a half-hour later.

"Look, gang, Susan's back," she heard a voice say and recognized it as Ann's.

Within the next moment, her girls had piled in through the door and gathered all around her bed, shouting and asking questions all at the same time. "How was your date?" "What did you do?" "What did you bring us?" "Do you like Jerry?"

Susan gazed at them and smiled, as she said, "Hold on there, one question at a time."

She related that she had a wonderful time but had not brought them anything since she hadn't gone to any stores. Bunk 6 insisted upon hearing the full story of the date and sat in Indian fashion around her bed. Susan couldn't refuse, so she related the day's adventures to listening children with eager faces.

When she finished, she asked what they had done and heard the good news. Marsha, one of Jerry's assistants, had given Janie, Ann, and Donna their beginning swimming tests, and they had all passed. Susan was pleased her campers had learned some of the fundamentals of swimming so quickly. Even though all the girls lived in the area around Miami, only Lynn had learned how to swim well before coming to camp. It was because of her previous swimming lessons that Lynn had become an intermediate swimmer on the first day of camp. Now, all of the girls, except Micky, could try to work toward passing their intermediate test before the summer ended. Micky was gradually overcoming her fear of water and was becoming more confident about learning how to swim.

One of camp's major events, the annual camp talent show, would take place in a week. Susan wanted to see her entire group on stage, but she especially hoped to persuade Janie to be in it. She had been surprised one night to hear Janie sing. Hers wasn't a childish voice but almost a mature, well-modulated voice. Janie, however, was fearful of singing before an audience. She would sing when she was by herself in some secluded place or while lying on her bed during rest hour when she thought the others weren't listening.

Susan decided it would be her project to convince Janie to perform Saturday night. While Janie preferred to be by herself rather than mix with others, Susan noticed that when forced into an activity or event, Janie would actually participate. Susan decided to push hard. She felt if this shy child was handled gently but firmly, with praise and encouragement, her lack of confidence would disappear. Donna had already told Susan that she would sing in the show, and Micky and Ann planned a small comedy act.

Susan sat quietly engulfed in her thoughts when she suddenly realized her girls had prepared for bed. She, too, was tired and decided that instead of walking to the lodge, she would also retire. Once her head hit the pillow, her mind filled with thoughts of Jerry and the talent show. Tomorrow, she planned to offer assistance to Mike to arrange the program. During former years, as a camper, she had always assisted counselors in planning their talent shows. Thus, she felt qualified. She considered ideas Mike might find useful. After all, a week didn't last long at camp. Unless they started preparing soon, there would not be enough time to present a good revue.

Her memories faded back to the night when she had sung in the talent show. It had been a wonderful evening. She had performed "I Can't Say No." Everyone in her cabin group had been impressed. In fact, they had told her she was one of the stars. That was a highlight of her camping years she pleasantly remembered as she fell asleep.

The following day, Tuesday, was a day Ann eagerly awaited. Every Tuesday and Friday, Bunk 6 had classes in arts and crafts. At the beginning of camp, they made drawings and poster paintings. However, after the optional sketch class had started, they worked on special projects instead. The girls had completed a number of different pieces this summer. They had made ceramic ashtrays and small paper scrapbooks bound in leather. The campers had drawn designs on the skin. Afterwards, Jean burned the designs onto the leather with the machine in the crafts building.

Before they could attend arts and crafts, they had to go to breakfast and have their cabin inspected. Inspections had been scored daily for a week. They totaled scores on Saturdays. The highest scoring cabin groups for both boys and girls received a plaque as well as ice cream treats of their choice at a nearby ice cream parlor. The cabins received grades from one to ten points. They received demerits for improperly made beds, unclean porches, messy bathrooms, sloppy cubbyholes, and poorly swept floors.

Although Susan's group remained cooperative in pitching in to get the work done and finishing before inspections, they weren't always as neat as they should be. Because of this, they had not won the plaque that first time. This week, Bunk 5 girls and Bunk 8 boys had the privilege of hanging the coveted plaques outside their cabin doors. However, Bunk 6 had worked hard since Sunday when weekly scores began again and had received high marks. They had received a "nine" and a "ten" out of ten.

After inspection, they went to what Jean called her "second home," arts and crafts. "Hi, people, are you prepared to start a new project today?" Jean asked Bunk 6.

Ann, excited about doing anything concerned with art, replied, "What are we making?"

Some of the girls shrugged their shoulders while others nodded "yes" in answer to Jean's question.

"Today, we will make something I think your mothers will like. Earrings. You will make earrings out of copper covered with enamel powder. You can choose any color and design you wish. This project usually takes from one to three hours so don't expect to finish it this session. It will involve hard work; however, when you're finished, you'll have something of which you can be proud." Jean proceeded to tell them where to get supplies which the girls enthusiastically gathered.

Donna happily announced, "At last, I'll have a chance to make a gift for my mother. Before I left, she reminded me, 'Don't forget to make something for me this summer.' I'd rather make earrings than do anything else. Wow! I thought I'd never get the chance to do it. This is great."

The campers worked slowly except for Ann who was skilled in crafts. Jean helped them every step of the way. She showed them how to shape and clean the copper. Since all the campers, except Ann, needed her help with each process, the others waited impatiently. They urged her to hurry with another camper despite Jean's assurances she would be with them as soon as possible. Susan frequently offered her assistance despite having the disadvantage of not having done this type of work before. When the period finished, Bunk 6 had completed several steps of the process including making crucial decisions as to what color and design they wanted their earrings to be enameled.

They would finish during the next arts and crafts class when they would place their earrings into a high-temperature kiln and watch the enamel fuse to the copper's surface. The last steps were cleaning the back of the copper and then affixing ear wires into place.

With five minutes of the period remaining, Jean told them to put their work away. She had assigned each bunk a different shelf in the arts and crafts building where they kept their projects. While the campers put their earrings on the shelf, Jean called Susan aside. "How is Lynn?" she asked.

"Lynn's fine. She'll be out of the infirmary tomorrow," Susan assured her.

Jean smiled and said, "I'm glad."

At last, the whistle blew indicating the change of activity. The girls left for archery class despite their many protests and requests to return to the cabin.

Susan interrupted, "No complaints, girls. You have learned a great deal in archery. Most of you are hitting the target with consistency. I think Marla has a surprise for you today."

"Big deal! Come on, Susan, all of us want to go back to the cabin," complained Micky.

"Micky, be quiet. What's the surprise, Susan?" piped up Donna. Donna, Susan noticed, had become more eager to participate in camp activities. During optional periods, she worked enthusiastically on the camp play.

"You'll see," Susan grinned. She led them to the archery range arriving about five minutes late.

"What took you so long?" Marla demanded angrily. "Let's get to work." Marla started the campers shooting at five targets set up on the archery range. She aggressively corrected how they shot. She turned to Susan, "Why don't you go to the lake and spend some time with Jerry? Maybe you should just drop in."

Susan ignored this and thought, "She really likes Jerry. Why should I be concerned? Jerry likes me. Besides, I'm occupied with the talent show and helping my girls. If she wants Jerry, why should I care?"

However, the truth was, although Susan did not want to admit it, she did care. She liked Jerry very much. She was thrilled that he wanted to date her instead of anyone else this summer. The campers weren't the only ones with problems and inner conflicts; counselors had them, too.

Marla continued to correct the girls harshly. It seemed to Susan that Marla was more critical today than she should have been. Was this her method of showing her jealousy of Susan? Susan didn't like it and called to Marla, "May I see you a moment?"

"Can't you see I'm busy?" Marla huffed and then mildly scoffed the campers for not being as good as her nine-year-olds. She continued to correct them severely.

"Marla, why don't you like Susan?" Janie was inquisitive.

"Keep on shooting. You are here to learn archery not to ask questions about my personal life. Besides, I have an announcement for all of you. Camp has a Robin Hood Division Contest. The best shooter from each cabin represents their group. I fully expect it to be you, Janie."

"What kind of contest will it be?" inquired Janie.

"Each age division has its own archery contest. The best shooter, the Robin Hood from that division, receives a trophy at the camp banquet. Your division consists of archers from the eight through eleven-year-olds. Senior division has twelve through fourteen-year-olds. If you want to be Robin Hood, you had better learn to shoot instead of talk."

"Marla, I'd like to see you for a minute privately." Susan was furious because of Marla's treatment of her campers.

"Obviously you won't stop nagging me until I do," Marla answered disdainfully. She appointed Janie the leader, and the two counselors walked over to some tall shade trees located a short distance from the campers.

Susan started, "Why are you acting this way? You are obviously jealous of my friendship with Jerry. Stop being so impossible when you are teaching my girls. Leave my campers out of our personal lives."

"I don't understand what you are talking about. I could care less if you dated Jerry," snapped Marla.

"Come on, Marla. Don't play games. I know what happened last year between you, Carol, and Jerry. So cool it and leave my kids alone."

Marla had a strange expression on her face as if she had been caught with her hand in the proverbial cookie jar. She thought to herself, "O.K., how will I get out of this?"

Susan continued, "I know you don't like me. Fine. I also know why. You know what? I don't care. I'm warning you, if you take it out on my campers again, I'll handle you my way. You can also keep in mind that I like Jerry. He's a great guy, so don't tell me any garbage about him."

Marla was speechless. She realized, at last, that someone was aware of the game she was playing. She thought to herself, "Susan isn't as dumb as she looks. Darn it." Without another word, she returned to her archery instruction and eased up on Susan's campers for the rest of the period.

Usually during rest hour, the counselors had a meeting with Mrs. Warren or took part in some activity such as riding or swimming. This was also when the CITs and junior counselors supervised campers. After lunch, during today's rest hour, Susan decided to talk with Mike about the talent show. He was on the stage in the rec hall painting scenery for the camp play to be held in less than two weeks.

"Hi," he greeted her and motioned for her to come to him. "Can I interest you in some painting? A lot of work needs to be done before we can call *South Pacific* a show."

"How is the talent show coming along?" asked Susan, as she grabbed a paintbrush.

"Fine. Why?"

"Do you want help with it? I used to help out with shows when I was a camper. I have a few suggestions. Besides, I need your help," admitted Susan.

"Sure, I need help because it is taking my time away from the big production. What's your problem?"

"Have you heard Janie sing? The kid is great. I want her to be in the talent show," insisted Susan.

"We can always put one more act in the show. However, we already have ten singers. I don't think it's wise to add too many more vocalists this year. In answer to your question though, I haven't heard her. Why didn't she come to see me when I made the announcement for auditions on Sunday?"

"That's the problem, Mike. She's too shy. Janie only sings when she thinks no one is listening. She has a natural talent."

"When I see her this afternoon, I'll speak to her about it. She's doing a great job as my assistant for the musical. I'm glad Mrs. Warren chose *South Pacific* this year since the campers are familiar with it. But I'm worried. They aren't developing as fast as I thought they would or should," complained Mike.

"Mike, that's the way it always seems with a camp musical. The acting comes together at the last moment. I know you are primarily interested in the play because that's the big event of the season. So let me help with the talent show. It will ease things for you. What can I do?"

"You can arrange the acts in the proper order and help me rehearse them. The show is this coming Monday. You're doing a great painting job," said Mike, admiring Susan's work on the scenery.

Susan was happy that Mike had agreed to talk to Janie. However, she wondered if it would do any good. Yet it might. Mike had been the one to convince Janie to be his assistant in producing the play when no one else could interest her in working with other people. Susan thanked him and wished him luck with his production before returning to her campers. She felt guilty not helping him more, but it was almost the end of rest hour.

After the day's activities were over, the campers prepared for bed. Susan asked Janie, "Are you in the talent show?"

She received a quizzical look for a reply.

"Janie, didn't Mike ask you to perform in the talent show next Monday?"

"I went briefly to today's rehearsal, Susan," Janie admitted while preparing for bed.

After lights out, Susan said good night to her campers and walked over to the lodge. She saw Mike signal for her to come over.

"Is Janie sick? She left rehearsal suddenly today," Mike inquired.

Susan seated herself next to him. "She was more quiet than usual at dinner and skit night. She told me, while she prepared for bed, that she only went briefly to rehearsal. Mike, do you know what's wrong? I mean, did you yell at her or did someone say anything about her being an assistant? I know her bunkmates are very proud of her."

"Wait a minute. I remember now." He paused and shook his head. "Of course," he sighed, "One of the older girls kidded her about being a ten-year-old ham. I thought Janie knew she was doing a good job. I've told her so myself. Janie is a sensitive girl, Susan. Too sensitive! Please try to explain to her that Linda was only teasing her. The more I think about it, I remember Janie was quiet at the beginning of today's rehearsal. She left as quickly as possible."

"I think we have a problem, Mike," Susan agreed. "Janie tries so hard to do something well. She is not skilled in arts and crafts or athletics except for archery. I think she was trying to do a good job helping you. When another camper criticized her, she became disappointed and displeased with herself. Criticism tends to throw her. She is creative in so many areas. Did you know she writes poetry?"

"No, I didn't," said Mike.

"I've been carrying around one that she gave me," said Susan. "Listen to this. It's really good." Susan then handed Mike the poem.

"The sea is green, but they say it's blue.

Softest gleam, softest hue.

Little sands on the beach

White as bleach."

"That kid is really talented," Mike said, "But she is an emotional egg shell. I hate to see her broken by idiots who don't think. Oh, well!" he exclaimed, shaking his head.

"If you'll excuse me, Susan," Mike added, "I want to work on some ideas for the musical. I have to plan how to get these kids to settle down and produce something worthwhile in a three-act play. See you later." He left the lodge.

"I see I have competition," declared a familiar voice.

Susan turned around and saw Jerry. "Hi. Don't be silly. We were discussing Janie," she greeted him.

"Mother Susan has another problem. Would you care to tell me about it?" he asked, as he sat on a chair facing her.

"Thanks, Jerry. I need a listening ear. It's Janie." She proceeded to tell him the story until he interrupted her.

"Susan, I agree that Janie needs a push. I had a cousin like her. She was so quiet and shy when she was a little older than Janie. The only way her parents could get her out with people or doing something which wasn't creative was through constant praise and encouragement. I noticed in swimming class that Janie wants to participate. However, I have to motivate her to go through the paces."

"But how, Jerry? How do I get her to perform in the talent show?" Susan inquired.

"Do her bunkmates like her voice?"

"They love it. Oh, they pretend they're not listening because she stops singing when she realizes they are paying attention. However, I've noticed they slow their games or whatever else they are doing when she starts," Susan pointed out.

"Remember. On our date, we discussed your campers and their different personalities. Let Micky encourage Janie's singing. Have her help you," he suggested.

"Jerry, that's a great idea. I think Micky will cooperate."

"Fine. Well, little mother," Jerry grinned, "since we have your huge problem solved, what about us?"

"What about us?"

"Do we have a date Monday?"

"Thanks for the advice, Jerry, but I can't. I'm sorry. That's talent show day. I promised Mike I would help him Monday afternoon with rehearsals. Please. No more on that subject," Susan said softly.

"Fine. I'll go along with you this time, but I think you're wrong to work so hard. I have OD tomorrow. However, I'm free Friday night. How about a drive and some pizza after taps?"

"That I'd like," Susan admitted.

"Fine," he repeated. "I'll meet you in front of the mess hall about 9:00. Good luck with Janie."

"Thanks. Good night, Jerry," Susan murmured as she left the lodge. The night air was cool. A flight of fireflies lent enchantment to her walk back to the cabin. She quickly undressed and lay down on her bunk. Before she fell asleep, Susan thought of Jerry. "I'm glad he understands me and respects my desire to spend the summer being a counselor and a date."

Before inspection the next morning, Susan asked Micky, who was sweeping first shift, to follow her outside the cabin for a moment.

Micky put away the broom, followed her onto the cabin patio, and asked, "Did I do anything wrong, Susan? I've been nice to Lynn since she got back. What did I do?"

Susan smiled, "Relax. I just need your help. It's true you girls are treating Lynn a little better since she returned from the infirmary. However, it's Janie that I want to talk about, Micky."

Micky looked puzzled. "What's wrong with Janie?"

"You've heard Janie sing. I think she should be in the talent show. Do you like her singing?"

"She's great. But what about the show, Susan?"

"Janie doesn't think anyone likes her singing."

"If she thinks like that, she's nuts," Micky interrupted.

"No. She doesn't have any confidence in herself, like you and the others have. She needs encouragement from people her own age," Susan said, staring directly at her camper, "Micky, do you understand what I want you to do?"

Micky shrugged. "Not really."

"If Janie hears praise coming from you, it will be more effective than if it came from me. If you encourage her by telling her what a good voice she has, you may help us to get her into the talent show. I think Janie, deep inside, wants to be in the show. She doesn't say so because she is half shy and half scared. Please tell Janie you like her voice," requested Susan.

"Oh, sure I'll do it," agreed Micky. "I'll get the others to help, too."

Susan thanked her and suggested they finish cleaning the cabin. Morning activities of softball, nature class, and general swim kept Bunk 6 occupied. Soon it was lunch, then rest hour.

During rest hour, Susan was at the rec hall speaking with Mike about the talent show lineup. Back at the cabin, Micky approached Janie.

"Hey, Janie, are you in the talent show?"

"Yeah, you ought to," commented Lynn. Since she had left the infirmary, she had been trying to be friendly toward the others. So far, she had rarely needled them or been sarcastic.

Janie looked up from the comic book she was reading. "What can I possibly do?" she asked.

"You can sing," pointed out Micky.

"Aw, come on. Give me a break. You have to be nuts to suggest that," muttered Janie.

"No, she's not," broke in Ann. "Do you think we haven't heard you? You're good."

"Ann, do you actually think I can sing?" responded Janie. She could not believe her ears. At last, someone thought she could do something well. "Hey, maybe I can sing," she thought, still unsure of her capabilities.

"You, turkey, what do you think we've been trying to tell you?" snapped Donna.

"Why don't you want to be in the show?" Micky pressed again. "The camp will think you're great. I know it."

"No, they won't. You only say that because you're my bunk-mates and because we've lived together for a few weeks. You've never heard me."

"Dummy, why don't you believe us? We have ears. We've heard you singing. However, if you don't want to be in the show, I guess that's your business," snarled Lynn impatiently.

"It is our business, Lynn," interrupted Micky. "We ought to have one decent act from our cabin. Ann, Donna, and I are in the talent show. We aren't half as talented as Janie. Please, Janie, be in the show."

"But I'm scared," whimpered Janie.

"Why are you scared? We're all your friends in this cabin. So are all the rest of the campers. Why should you be afraid to sing in front of your friends?" prodded Micky, taking a deep breath and getting a little disgusted. "After all, how can one kid be so messed up?" she wondered.

"Sure," agreed Lynn. "Look. You're the assistant of the play. You could be the big wheel of the talent show if you're in it."

"Hi, girls," called out Susan, walking through the door and dismissing the CIT who was diligently reading a recent issue of *National Enquirer*.

"Susan, don't you think Janie should be in the talent show?" asked Donna.

"Definitely. How about it, Janie? By the way, I saw Mike. He missed talking to you at rehearsals yesterday, and he wants you there today. Besides, I told him about your singing. He wants to hear you. I think you're good enough to be in the talent show. I'll bet you'll be the best act of all."

Janie stared hard at Susan before quickly rolling over on her bunk bed to face the wall, "You didn't. Oh, Susan, you didn't."

Susan climbed on the child's bed and put her arm around her. "Janie, come on now. I'm sure everyone in camp would like to hear you sing in the talent show. You don't have to unless you want to. However, I'd like you to try out for Mike. Please, do it for me."

Janie calmed down and agreed to audition for Mike. This was immediately greeted by happy and proud shouts from her bunkmates. Janie might be persuaded to be in the show after all. Surprisingly, even Lynn was not sarcastic as she might have been before the accident. She joined in with the others to celebrate Janie's decision.

After rest hour, during the rehearsal of *South Pacific*, Mike addressed Janie. "Why didn't you stay yesterday? Do you intend to let teasing get under your skin?" He gave her a hug and added, "Janie, you're a great girl and a big help with our play. Don't forget it."

"Mike, do you think we'll be ready on time?" inquired Janie, trying to change the subject.

"It depends. If we all work hard, I think we can do it; otherwise, no. Susan wants you to sing in the talent show on Monday. How about trying out for me?"

"Do you think we are working hard enough?" Janie asked, making another attempt to avoid auditioning for Mike.

"Janie, what's the problem? You are my coaching assistant for the play. That's harder than being in the talent show. I promise the audience will be friendly. Now come on, Janie, sing."

Janie couldn't refuse anymore and sang a Broadway tune. When she was through, there was applause from all the other campers in the rec hall.

Mike smiled and insisted, "You're good. In fact, I think you would be marvelous in the show. So you're in it." He started the afternoon's rehearsal.

When Janie returned to the cabin and told her bunkmates the news, everyone was pleased. However, they had expected as much. Mike had a way with Janie. He knew how to get her out of her shell.

At the lodge that night, Susan waved Mike over. "Just wanted to thank you for persuading Janie. How on earth did you ever convince her?" she greeted him.

"Well," he said, "I tried to give Janie some confidence and would only take 'yes' for an answer. You were right. She has some voice."

The two counselors sat planning arrangements for the talent show. A musical show singer would start the show. Janie would be the last number on the program. In between, other singers, comedians, dancers, pianists, a trumpet player, and two guitarists would perform. They thought it would be an excellent program. Mike was glad at least one show looked promising.

Susan held rehearsals for the talent show on Sunday. Everyone was cued to make certain they knew when to make their entrance. Jerry wandered into the rec hall. Convinced that Susan wouldn't change her mind and take her day off away from camp, he invited her for a moonlight canoe ride after taps. This, she quickly accepted.

At last, it was their moment. Evening activities had ended, and the campers were in bed. They strolled to the waterfront and then eased one of the canoes off the racks and into the lake. They paddled slowly toward the middle of the lake where they talked as the canoe drifted.

"Susan," Jerry whispered. "you know that I'm crazy about you. I don't know how to break you of your being so darn diligent about your job. I want to spend all of our spare time together."

"I know, Jerry, I feel the same way. But I love my job, and sometimes it has to come first. Please understand."

They paddled toward shore and beached the canoe. Walking back to the lodge, hand-in-hand, they stopped and warmly kissed. Susan returned to her cabin where she found all her campers sleeping soundly. She decided to do the same.

At last, it was Monday, talent show day. Excitement brewed in the cabin from the moment Bunk 6 awoke. The same spirit followed them through lineup until the last preparations for the show including a final rehearsal. At 4:00 p.m., Susan and Mike reminded each camper in the show to bring his or her props to the rec hall. Everyone who would be performing wished each other luck and rushed around backstage in a flurry. It seemed as if they could hardly wait for the show to begin. Still, some of the participants admitted they were scared. At dinner, Bunk 6 discussed only the talent show.

Lynn had tried to make friends with the girls in her cabin. However, they continued to ignore her and didn't invite her to join them in their games or secrets. She felt left out. Susan told her that friendship was something that grew, and she should continue to give of herself. Once you lost a person's friendship, it was hard to regain it. Susan also told her not to give up the battle but to keep pitching. As soon as the others were convinced Lynn had changed, they would change also. Tonight, Lynn decided maybe she would show Bunk 6 she cared by serving as the group's cheerleader.

"Aren't you excited, Donna?" asked Lynn, enthusiastically. "I bet you will all be great."

"Boy, am I. I can hardly wait to sing. I hope I do all right," replied Donna, breathlessly.

"Ann, you had better remember your lines," prompted Micky.

"I'll remember. Don't you forget yours either. What's the matter, Janie?" Ann seemed puzzled at Janie's silence.

"Nothing. Susan, do I have to go through with this? I don't want to."

"You'll do fine. You're only experiencing stage fright which is a natural thing. Don't worry. Remember what Mike and I have been trying to tell you. We are all your friends," Susan reminded her.

"You'll all do fantastically. I can't wait to see your acts," cheered Lynn.

At last, they finished dinner. Ann, Donna, and Micky ran ahead to get into their costumes so as to be ready with time to spare. The show would start in a half hour. Excitement reigned high, yet Janie seemed withdrawn. Susan again gave her gentle encouragement and told her to hurry and get ready.

All over the cabin, Susan's girls had tossed their clothes. Even though it looked as if a tornado had hit, she forgot to scold her campers.

Those appearing in the show hurried to get backstage. They sat on the provided benches. Mike ordered them to be quiet as the rest of the camp piled into the rec hall to sit at their assigned places.

The show started. Mike stepped out in front of the curtain and welcomed everyone to the fourth annual Camp Floridian talent show. He introduced the first act, a fourteen-year-old girl who sang a number from one of the hit Broadway shows. Act after act moved along smoothly. At last, it was Janie's turn to perform.

She started hesitantly, then warmed up and sang beautifully. The audience listened intently until she finished. A wave of applause resounded through the whole rec hall. No one had known Janie Barnes had such a terrific voice. Afterwards, Mike closed the show by having all the performers and Susan come out from behind the curtain for a final bow. The campers hurried from the stage to be with their bunkmates and ask their counselors how they liked the show.

"Janie," Lynn shouted, hugging her. "You were great. You were the best act in the whole show."

Her other bunkmates heaped praise on her, and Susan was elated. Other campers came over to Janie to tell her she was one of the evening's stars. To add to the excitement and fun, all the campers and counselors received ice cream sundaes for refreshments.

Janie felt warm inside. For the first time in her life, she believed she had done something worthwhile. She could barely enjoy her sundae because of the inner thrill she was experiencing from tonight's success. Now, she might come out of her shell. When she prepared for bed, she was too excited to sleep.

Before Susan left her campers, she told each of her charges who had been in the show that they had been excellent. Janie clung to Susan and then looked up smiling. She seemed unable to contain her emotions. It was one of the few times she had been so happy that summer. Her pillow felt cool against her cheek, and she gradually drifted off to sleep with a smile.

Chapter Nine

Camp Floridian's Broadway Show

Susan did not have an opportunity to see Jerry until after breakfast the following morning. "Hi," Jerry greeted Bunk 6 with a smile when they arrived for their swimming class.

"Ah, here's the talent show star," he added, looking at Janie. "I've heard all about you."

"Thanks," said Janie shyly, responding to Jerry's compliment with a slow grin.

The girls started to work on the breaststroke. They were serious about learning how to swim. It was a hot day, and the water felt cool and refreshing. Due to Jerry's constant encouragement, even Micky was now willing to participate in swimming classes. However, Micky worked with Theresa, one of Jerry's assistants, since she was on a different skill level than the others.

Jerry enjoyed being around children as much as Susan did. However, it was his opinion counselors should have a little fun and not work seven days a week. He believed it necessary to take advantage of assigned days off and decided to speak to Susan about this. At the period's end, he motioned for her to come over. "Can I see you alone for a few moments?" he asked.

"Sure, Jerry. What's up?" Susan inquired. They strode away from the campers.

"I didn't see you at the lodge last night. Is everything all right?"

"Sure. Working on the show exhausted me, and I went to bed early," explained Susan.

"Susan, listen. I like you very much, and you're a good counselor. But it's abnormal not to want to take a day off. You should have some fun this summer. Remember, all work and no play makes for a dull girl. Since I don't want you to ruin your shine, let's go out next Monday."

Taken back for a moment, Susan paused and calmly said, "I'd love to go out on Monday, but please remember, Jerry, my work is important to me, too. Sometimes I need to put it before anything else. I don't want to discuss this anymore."

He shook his head. "I'm sorry. I hate to see you work so hard, but all right, subject closed."

Susan collected her girls, and they started back to the cabin. Janie and Donna went to rehearsals while the others ambled off to their regular camp activities.

Excitement had died down around camp after last night's talent show although some campers and counselors continued to talk about it. The big news was the camp musical that would take place Saturday night, followed a week later by Visitors Day. Mike held rehearsals for the play during second, third, and fourth periods. The campers worked hard, but they didn't accomplish as much as Mike had hoped.

It was now Tuesday, five more days before the big show. Mike was heard mumbling to himself, "How on earth will these kids be ready Saturday when they continue to fool around?"

Janie collected the props needed for *South Pacific* while diligently working during rehearsals on recording stage directions. Mike had also asked her to be the play's prompter. She carefully wrote changes in the dialogue during rehearsals and called out lines when the actors forgot them. Janie could sense Mike's tensions concerning the show and shared them with him. She wanted to shout to the others to remember their lines and work toward a successful show.

Today's rehearsals seemed disorganized. The campers had recently started learning the third act. With dress rehearsals starting in two days, Mike kept his fingers crossed. He still had his doubts everything would come together despite assurances from other counselors who had stopped in to watch from time to time.

At lunch, Lynn asked Janie, "How is the play coming?"

"I guess we're doing all right," Janie hesitated. "We're on the third act. Mike had hoped we'd be finishing it by now. Gosh, for Mike's sake, I hope we do a good job."

Lynn responded, "Why don't you tell him to stop worrying? With Mike directing, you'll do fine. If it is as good as the talent show was, it will be great."

"I hope so, Lynn, but he won't stop worrying until Saturday night is over," Janie sighed. "I can't tell him to relax."

"Aw stick it. I was only trying to make a suggestion," pouted Lynn.

"I have one to make. Why don't you shut up, Lynn," sneered Micky. She, more than anyone else in the group, had doubts Lynn would change. She still mistrusted Lynn's intentions.

"Now, girls, especially you, Micky, let's not squabble. Of course, the play will be wonderful. I can't wait to see it," added Susan, attempting to restore peace to Bunk 6.

She diverted their attention by bringing up a new subject: the campout planned for the camp season's fifth week. For their overnight, they would walk to a site located about a mile from camp. Everyone eight years and older went on a trip. Two or three cabin groups always camped at the same time sharing fun and responsibilities. During campcraft, the children learned such skills as using sleeping bags, building a fire, and cooking food out-of-doors. It was on the overnight trip that knowledge of these skills came into actual practice. This was one of the major seasonal events to which campers anxiously looked forward.

For the rest of the day, rehearsals went smoothly with the actors completing the third act's other half. Mike was amazed. At last, they had started to wake up and work. Although the cast members weren't very optimistic, they were also not completely discouraged. A strong possibility existed that the show might be a success.

That evening at dinner, the discussion focused on the group's daily accomplishments. Lynn had water-skied halfway around the lake. This was a feat not easily accomplished by children less than thirteen years of age since the lake was about a two mile run. Ann had drawn another landscape and kept showing improved talent.

All of a sudden, the girls started whispering as they received dessert. Susan glanced at them. "What's up, girls?"

"Oh, nothing," chuckled Micky, giving the signal.

Bunk 6 shouted in unison as loud as they possibly could, "Susan and Jerry sitting in a tree k-i-s-s-i-n-g. First comes love. Then comes marriage. Then comes Susan with a baby carriage."

Susan turned bright red as everyone in the mess hall turned around. She had an instantaneous desire to dive under the table. However, she suppressed her wish, glared at her girls, and said, "Cute."

Shortly afterwards, they left the building to return to their cabin to dress for Capture the Flag, the night's activity. Following the game, after putting her charges to bed, Susan decided to go to the lodge. She wandered over slowly, enjoying the brisk breeze blowing off the lake. She entered, sat on one of the rockers, and started reading *Parents* magazine while waiting for Jerry.

At the lodge, to her surprise, Marla wandered over to her. "I forgot to tell you what a terrific job you did with the talent show," she commended Susan. "I heard you were Mike's assistant. I guess I underestimated your capabilities."

"Thanks, Marla. I did very little work. The credit goes to Mike."

"That's not what I heard. And Janie was terrific. I didn't know she is as good a singer as she is an archer. You have a group of good kids. They made themselves heard at dinner," she laughed.

"Yes, they did," responded Susan, trying not to show her amazement at Marla's sudden display of pleasantry. As Marla strolled away, she wondered what had softened her. Perhaps, Marla, like Lynn, was trying to improve her personality. However, adults don't change overnight. Susan was skeptical and thought, "What is Marla's new approach? I don't understand it."

Jerry later joined her. "Hi. Except for dinner," he shook his head and grinned, "how did everything go for the rest of the day?"

"Fine. Janie has a new problem. She's concerned about Mike and the show. In fact, that's all my girls have been discussing."

"Interested in boys at her age? She ought to leave that to you," he teased, his blue eyes smiling at her. "I guess everyone is concerned about the play. My boys are sailors in it. I think I have the song 'There is Nothing Like a Dame' coming out of my ears."

"It ought to be a good show. Hey there's Mike. Mike," she called.

"I may start to get jealous," he teased her again. "Imagine showering your attention on a theater major when you could have a handsome doctor."

"Relax, Doc. I only want to see how the play is coming along."

"Hi, Mike. How's everything?" she asked when he had joined them.

"The cast showed improvement today. I guess there's still hope. Susan, I told Janie she was one of the stars last night. What a voice!"

They talked about counseling, shows, and children in general before saying good night. This was Mike's third year as a counselor. He enjoyed teaching children drama and being in charge of evening activities and Color War.

At Camp Floridian, Color War was to be held for five days during the sixth week of camp. Everyone would be divided into two teams, the blues and the whites. The only exceptions were Mrs. Warren, Mike, Mitzi, and Ted. They would decide who would be on what team, so as to make the two teams as equal as possible, and serve as judges of every contest. The teams would eat together throughout the War. Even inspection would be graded with demerit points being taken off the teams' scores.

The leaders of both teams chose athletes for every event. Points would be awarded to winners and those placing second and third. On the first day, they held a swimming meet in the afternoon. During the morning of the second day, contests continued in archery, riflery, jacks (for the junior girls), tetherball (for the junior boys), and tennis. A softball game took place in the afternoon. On the third day, campers participated in a rodeo in the morning and a football game during the afternoon. The campers had soccer games for both boys and girls, on the fourth day, as well as a rehearsal for the big sing to be held the following day. On the fifth day, the various songs presented received prized points. Each team had its their own cheer, razz song, pep song, and alma mater graded for originality and creativity. Teams marched their wall plaques, for which they received points, into the rec hall. The Sing, every year, always seemed to determine the winner. Color War at Camp Floridian was the time when healthy competition and sportsmanship played key roles of camp life.

On Thursday, dress rehearsals for *South Pacific* started. Janie did not go to any regular activities nor did anyone else associated with the play. She spent all her time except for meals, evening activity, and rest hour at the rec hall.

Mike cracked the whip constantly, yelling, "You should know your lines by now. How on earth do you expect to put on a decent presentation Saturday night?"

Each cast member went over scenes repeatedly so perfection might be achieved. Mike's uneasiness was contagious to those around him. All but a few wondered if the musical would be a success even though the cast worked hard. Excitement built to a fevered pitch where everyone's nerves reached the breaking point. At last, Saturday night arrived.

South Pacific had been the main topic of conversation around camp, for campers and counselors, for several days. Janie had hardly slept or eaten for two days because of her excitement and worries about the play's success. Immediately after the talent show, she had come out of her shell. Now she hid deep inside of it. However, Susan did not worry this time since she realized excitement sometimes caused tension. This was what Janie was experiencing.

The time for raising the stage curtain grew closer until 7:30 arrived. Everyone settled in the rec hall seats. Loud and noisy conversations between counselors and campers suddenly ceased when Mike walked out onto the stage. He could only hope for an excellent performance. Rehearsals had ended, and the show was about to begin.

"Campers. Counselors. Tonight Camp Floridian presents the fourth annual camp musical. We are presenting Rodgers and Hammerstein's *South Pacific* which we hope you will all enjoy." He stepped to the rec hall upright piano and played an overture from the show's best-known songs. The stage curtain rose and Act One began.

Janie, before curtain time, had discharged her duties as camper director. When the curtains opened, she sat in the wing ready to prompt any actor who forgot his lines. Her work had been extremely important during the last few weeks, and she eagerly awaited the results.

The play proceeded without any noticeable errors on the part of the cast. It was now intermission between the first and second acts. While the scenery changed, Mike went backstage to give the actors encouragement.

"I told you before we started tonight that I felt you would do all right. I didn't say that I thought you would do well or even great. I will say it now. If you continue to perform as you did during the first act, we will present the finest show this camp has ever seen."

He took the time to talk to individual actors who had important roles: praising them, giving them constructive criticism, or reminding them how to perform during certain scenes in the play's last half. Before the intermission ended, when the audience returned to their seats, he again addressed the entire cast.

"Keep it up, people. Good luck. I know you'll do well. Now go out there and show them what you can do."

Mike introduced the second act and the musical continued. In the audience, Ann turned to Susan, "Gee, what was Janie so worried about? Donna has sung well in the chorus. Don't you think it's a great play?"

"It's fabulous," commented Lynn.

"Who asked you?" Micky asked dryly. Susan told her to settle down and watch the show.

Mike crossed his fingers when the girl playing the role of Nellie didn't remember one of her lines. She forgot to look toward Janie, as the cast had been instructed to do, and made a feeble attempt to ad-lib. The show continued. At another time, a prop did not get on the stage in time and excitement loomed backstage. This error went unnoticed.

When the musical ended, it was well received. They called the performers out for two curtain calls. The cast and audience chanted repeatedly, "We Want Mike." He finally came to the stage's front and took his bow. Cheers and loud applause resounded from all sides of the rec hall.

Mike finally held up his hand and responded, "Thank you very much. We're glad you enjoyed it. How about some extra applause for some of our play's stars?" He called out, one by one, actors and actresses who had portrayed major roles.

"Weren't they great?" he added. "Let's hear it for them." He led the applause, which once more echoed through the building.

The curtain closed, and everyone in the audience filed out of the rec hall toward their cabins. As the cast members assembled backstage to congratulate each other and gather their different costumes, Mike announced, "We'll have a cast party in fifteen minutes so change into jeans and hurry back. I think you all deserve it. You were terrific. You don't know how pleased I am with you."

Donna and Janie rushed to catch up with the rest of Bunk 6 walking toward their cabin. But instead of Janie stopping when she had caught them, she raced ahead into the cabin, scrambled onto her bunk bed, and started sobbing into her pillow. When Susan reached the cabin, she went over to her camper and told the other girls to play a game for a while. She climbed upon Janie's bed, located directly over hers. She sat next to the child and gently touched her shoulder.

"Janie, what's wrong?" she asked.

"Nothing. Leave me alone."

"I thought you did a wonderful job with the play." Louder sobbing interrupted Susan. "The show was one of the best I've ever seen. Didn't you hear what Mrs. Warren said? She said that in her four years of running a camp, it was the finest performance of all. Now what's the matter?"

"If I...nothing," wept Janie, as if her heart would break.

"If what, Janie? Come on. Tell me. Aren't you feeling well?" She felt the child's forehead. Janie didn't have a fever.

"Susan, if I did so well, how come Mike didn't call me out for a bow?" Janie pointed out. She had stopped crying, but the tears glistened on her face.

"Janie, you did as well as any of the others. What would happen if Mike called everyone out for a separate bow? Wouldn't that be something?"

"Hey, Janie, hurry up for the cast party," prodded Donna. "What's wrong?" she asked when she had taken a quick look at Janie's face.

"I'm not going to any old party."

"What?" asked Susan, getting down from Janie's bed. "Don't tell me you want to miss a party?" Her answer was a renewed burst of tears.

"Should I wait?" asked Donna.

"No, go on. Janie will be there soon," Susan answered. "Have a good time." She noticed Micky and Ann playing jacks together while Lynn curled up on her bunk reading comics.

"Why don't you all play together, Lynn?"

"They don't want me to play with them so I won't," Lynn grumbled and returned to reading her comics.

"Micky, Ann, why not?"

"Because she cheats. That's why." Micky said indignantly.

"I do not. You only want to play by yourselves. Don't call me a cheater, you dirty liar," Lynn returned, as she jumped off her bed prepared to fight.

"Well, you do cheat, and I'm not a liar." Micky also scrambled to her feet.

Susan stepped between them and put an arm on each. "What do you think you are doing? Girls don't fight. Animals do. Now stop it, both of you. If you want to play jacks, all three of you will play or no one will. Understand?"

She let them cool off, glaring at each other. Ann had continued to play jacks, not wishing to be on either side. The two girls stomped away from each other, and Lynn stormed outside the cabin. Susan turned her attention back to Janie.

"Susan, why wasn't I called out on stage?" Janie moaned.

"Janie, what others may think and whether or not they called you to get applause may seem important to you now. They're not as vital as something else. Do you think you did a good job? That's what counts. Your bunkmates and I think you did an excellent job, and we're proud of you. Now, why don't you go to the cast party? You'll get there just in time."

The child finally agreed. She wiped her tears and hurried off to the cast party to be with Donna and the others.

"Janie, I've been looking all over for you," Mike greeted her, with a hug, when she walked into the rec hall. "You were a wonderful assistant. I don't think I could have directed the play without your help. Why don't you help yourself to some refreshments? There may even be some ice cream left."

Janie wandered over to the table where piles of food lay. A feeling of gaiety had replaced the earlier tension. Everyone was busy congratulating each other and saying, "I'm glad that's over. Isn't this a cool party?"

"Anything for food," said one of the boys who had been a sailor.

Not long after Janie arrived, the cast party broke up. Everyone returned quietly to their cabins. Mike had warned them to keep their voices low with the youngest children asleep; so conversations ended as soon as the campers left the rec hall.

When Janie and Donna reached their cabin, the others good-naturedly teased them. "To be in a play just to be able to go to a party when it's over, that's disgraceful," teased Micky.

"Yeah, they haven't gone to archery or campcraft for the past week, and they're rewarded for it. We should be given a party, instead, for having to spend time with Marla," pointed out Ann.

Susan had forgotten all about Marla. Marla seemed to be a changed person recently. She no longer used Bunk 6's campers as a target for her feelings toward Susan. She wondered, "What has happened to have changed Marla? Is she being pleasant for a reason or is she actually trying to change her personality?"

While the girls prepared for bed, they discussed the campout taking place in a few days. It would be fun sleeping and eating in the open air. They would sing before sleeping in front of a campfire. In the morning, surrounded by tall oaks and pines which seemed to reach clear up to touch the sky, they would cook an early breakfast over hot coals. Susan had seen the site and could hardly wait for the trip because she enjoyed camping in the out-of-doors.

When she was a child, her family had gone on summer expeditions in national parks and forests during the years that she and her brothers had not gone to camp. She could clearly remember the fishing, the charcoal-broiled food, the evening campfires, and the smell of pines and early morning air mingling together into a woodsy fragrance.

These remained some of her favorite memories of her childhood and young teens. She hoped Bunk 6 would like the campout also, and she made plans to help them enjoy themselves. Four more days remained until a night of fun, and only two more until another wonderful day off with Jerry. With Janie's problem resolved, Susan managed to sleep peacefully.

Chapter Ten

Another Date with Jerry

Sunday night, after her girls had fallen asleep, Susan roamed over to the lodge to spend time with the other counselors and talk shop. She had started realizing a good counselor doesn't necessarily spend all of her time with campers but saves part of the day for her own fun. It was important to be with people her own age.

Susan wanted to spend the evening with Jerry. She had found him to be a good friend and a wonderful guy. He helped her when she had a problem, shared her happiness, and cheered her when she was feeling blue.

When she reached the lodge, Susan saw Jerry sitting on the doorway's top step surveying the starry sky. He greeted her with, "It looks like we'll have clear skies for our date tomorrow. Do you want to go swimming?"

"Sure. I'd love it," replied Susan. "I enjoy swimming, especially at the beach. Salt water is the greatest."

"If you like swimming so much, why don't you come to the lake during rest hour more often? It's warm and relaxing there, too," he asked.

"Jerry, are you sure you don't want to be a salesman instead of a doctor? You'd be fabulous. First, you convince me to take a day off away from my kids," Susan teased, smiling at him. "Now, you are persuading me to enter your own special environment. You know what? You may have succeeded."

"I wasn't trying to be a salesman," he denied. "When I want something, I go after it. Besides, I don't think I've sold you yet on joining me whenever you aren't with your crew. I've got competition in Mike."

"Don't be jealous. I was only helping him with the shows. There's nothing serious between us. I only care about you, silly. Too bad we're not back home in Miami or I'd pack a picnic lunch."

"I'll take you up on your offer when we get home," he grinned. "I'll see you tomorrow. Same time. Same place."

"Rec hall?"

"No, at the mess hall right after cleanup. Well, see you then. I think I'll turn in. I'm bushed." He yawned, stood up, and gave her a quick kiss before strolling in the direction of the boys' cabins.

"Good night, Jerry," Susan called. "See you tomorrow." She entered the lodge to sit and chat with some other counselors. She talked with Mike about *South Pacific* and with Jean about the other crafts projects her group would do, before returning to her own cabin.

The following morning, they dressed in their bathing suits and left camp immediately after inspection. The scenery flew past as they drove toward the ocean. The oak trees resembled stately old men with beards since grey Spanish moss hung from their branches. The sky was pale blue with only a few, scattered, fluffy white clouds. Occasionally, they passed cattle ranches with herds of Brahma bulls. It was a beautiful day. No one could argue with that.

"Jerry, isn't it a peaceful day? It's perfect for heading to the beach and getting a sun tan," Susan announced.

"I agree. I can see those waves coming to the tips of the shore and then scurrying back again, leaving damp, cool sand behind."

"Ann would say, 'I'd love to paint the waves.' I want to think about what you said. If you get tired of being a doctor, and you don't want to be a salesman, you could always be a poet," Susan smiled, turning to look at him.

"Don't start that again," laughed Jerry. "I don't want to consider what I said, Susan. I want to concentrate on you. Did anyone ever tell you how pretty you are?"

"Jerry, thank you. Come on, no flattery."

"Did I say anything wrong? I meant what I said. You are the prettiest girl in camp. As I've told you before, you also happen to be one of the best counselors. I'm glad you're finally realizing being a top counselor doesn't mean one who spends all her time with her campers. I used to think I'd have to rope you away from those kids."

"I only stayed at camp on one of my days off. However, I appreciate your concerns. You're sweet."

"Thank you and thank you, again. No kidding, Susan, work is important, but it has its time and place. I'm sure that during the school year, you don't slave over your books every free moment or through every weekend. At least, I hope you don't. I want to see you when we return home, so please don't bury yourself in your books next semester."

"I'm looking forward to being with you, too, Jerry. I agree life consists of fun as well as work. However, I also think, and I believe in this strongly, work should be finished before play begins."

"Definitely," agreed Jerry. "My date is not only pretty but intelligent. What a combination!"

They became quiet, absorbed in scenery, while listening to the radio.

"Jerry, I'm puzzled about something. Marla has changed recently."

"In what way?"

"She's been friendly and easier on my kids. I don't understand it."

"Did you call her at her game?" he asked, glancing over at her.

"I think so. She shouted at my girls one day at archery, and I took her aside. I told her I was wise to her and to stop chewing out my girls because she didn't like me. I also informed her that she needn't tell me anything bad about you because I wouldn't believe her."

"What did she say?"

"She didn't answer. She just had a strange expression on her face. Since that time, she has changed her attitude toward my campers and me."

"Knowing Marla, I don't know what to believe. Maybe she has discovered she can't win or she might have some strategy up her sleeve. The important thing is I like you or I wouldn't ask you out. Please remember that," he remarked, as he drove on toward the ocean.

"I know, Jerry. However, she's changed and so suddenly."

Jerry shook his head and glanced over at her once more. "Let's forget about Marla and enjoy ourselves. I don't think we should be concerned about her any longer."

At last, they arrived at the ocean near Cocoa Beach. The salt water was inviting. Susan looked forward to getting wet. They took sun screen, towels, a beach blanket, and Jerry's transistor radio out of the convertible's trunk and placed them on the blanket near the water. After they applied sun screen, they ran together, hand in hand, toward the ocean. Suddenly Jerry dropped Susan's hand and dove into the waves.

"Get wet," he called to her. "The water is great." He splashed her.

The water revived them after the long hot drive, and the two swam together at first. As hard as Susan tried, she couldn't keep pace with Jerry's long, smooth strokes. After a half hour, they rested for a few moments before wading back to shore. They scrambled out of the water, dried themselves briskly, and fell onto the blanket, laughing gaily. It was fun, and they were enjoying themselves tremendously.

"Jerry Martin, Olympic swimming star. The greatest," shouted Susan. She ducked under a huge beach hat.

"Just for that, you get an honest to goodness drenching," Jerry warned. He rose as if in preparation to pick her up, then leaned over and kissed her lightly. "You know you're special."

He lay beside her and held her in a warm embrace. "I mean it, Susan. I think I'm falling in love with you." They kissed long and hard.

Susan gazed at him with a tender smile. Her heart beat rapidly. She was about to overflow with happiness. They stretched out on the blanket, with Susan's head on Jerry's chest, and listened to the radio playing soft instrumental music. The world was at peace, and everything was perfect.

"Hey, Susan," said Jerry, after they had soaked up the sun's rays for an hour. "I don't know about you, but beaches always make me hungry. In fact, I'm starved. I know a place for lunch where people come dressed as they are. The food isn't bad at all."

"Lead on," Susan agreed. "I'm ready to go." A short distance down the beach, they found restrooms where Jerry and Susan changed into shirts and shorts. After placing their swimsuits and the rest of their gear in the trunk, they headed for a restaurant about a half hour away.

"This place isn't luxurious," he warned, "and it doesn't look like much from the outside. But, don't let appearances fool you. Inside, it has a certain charm and the best barbecue I have ever eaten. Do you like barbecue? If you don't, we can go somewhere else."

"I love it. Jerry Martin, are you insinuating that I judge a book by its cover?" Susan teased.

"You're something else." Jerry looked over at her with admiration. After a few more miles, he slowed down and parked at a weather-beaten building that looked like it had seen better days.

Susan glanced at the restaurant's exterior and asked hesitantly, "Here?"

"If you don't like it here, we'll go somewhere else."

Susan quickly interrupted. "No, this is fine. I'm sure they have good food."

"Are you sure? I want you to be happy. I'm thinking of another place you may like better. It is about a fifteen-minute ride from here. They don't specialize in barbecue. They do serve good home-cooked meals."

Susan shook her head. "This is fine. Let's go inside so I can see that certain charm you told me about."

The interior was decorated in country style. Royal blue and white checked curtains hung at the windows with the room having pine paneling throughout. Fresh-cut flowers were placed at every table. A small stone fireplace stood at one end opposite the kitchen doors. The waitresses wore navy checked aprons over their starched white uniforms. The restaurant had a cozy atmosphere that immediately made you feel at ease.

Jerry ordered two barbecued chicken and ribs combination platters that came with creamy coleslaw, steak fries, and hot garlic bread. The service was excellent, another feature Jerry had mentioned.

While munching on ribs, Susan slowly grinned. "You know what? You were right. They have wonderful food here. How did you know about this place?"

"I came here frequently, last year, on my day off. I remembered this restaurant because when my family lived in this area, we ate here quite often. On the outside, it looks older and could probably use a paint job, but the inside has remained the same. I ate here last week."

"How do you know about all these dining rooms?"

"Only about ten casual eating places are in this immediate area and one very formal dining room. A jacket and tie place. So, it's easy to know about them."

They continued eating, and Jerry signaled the waitress over. He ordered a renewal of their ice teas. As they finished their meal, Susan looked long and hard at him, sighed, then softly said, "Jerry, there's one thing you haven't told me about yourself. Why did you decide to become a doctor? Don't tell me if you think it's too personal."

He grinned at her. "Is that all you want to know? That's not too personal. There's a story about it. I lived on a farm and was always interested in how living things functioned. My mother used to say that when I was a boy, I hung around the kitchen. But, before she had a chance to cook chicken, I would examine it. I guess I wanted to know how it was constructed. I used to examine rabbits, pigs, and horses. Once, a horse kicked me while I was doing that. It didn't stop my interest in animals. My father became convinced that the only way to prevent me from getting kicked in the head would be to buy me a book on anatomy. He was a country doctor. My interest grew from anatomy to other phases of medicine. At last, I knew what I wanted to become."

"A veterinarian?" interrupted Susan.

"When I was younger, I thought about being a vet. Now, I want to be a pediatrician. Med school is rough though, and I hear internship is no joy ride either."

"You still want to become a doctor?"

"Definitely. It's as important to me as children are to you. I don't think my life would be complete without medicine. You know how some people feel medicine or priesthood or some other career is their special calling. Well, that's the way I am." He paused for a moment. "That's enough about me. You never told me what career you are planning, Susan."

"I don't know. I seriously considered becoming a teacher when I was younger. I"m majoring in psychology, but I haven't decided on a career."

"Maybe, with your interest in kids, you could be a guidance counselor or even a psychologist," Jerry commented. "Well, let's go. We need time to get some goodies for your campers."

They left the restaurant and headed south along the coast. They planned to go west to Orlando and back to camp. Susan had been given money, by the girls in Bunk 6, for comic books and candy. It would be a simple matter to buy these items in a city as large as Orlando.

"Susan," admitted Jerry, after they had traveled for a distance. "I'm glad we did this today. I enjoy every moment I'm with you."

"Jerry, I feel the same way about you. Thanks for understanding why I turned you down last week. This has been fun."

"I'm glad you're having a good time. I think you know that I want to spend a lot of time with you this summer. I can't believe how quickly the last few weeks have passed, and I want us to take advantage of any time we have left."

"Does the season always go so fast?"

"Not really. Last year, it seemed to drag. If it hadn't been for my group of boys, I would have had a miserable summer. You know, we have an excellent group of campers this year with the nine- and ten-year-olds. Some counselors have nothing but spoiled brats. Your kids are terrific."

"Yes, I do have a good group. They still have a few problems. However, these are being ironed out. Donna, at first, was homesick. After she became interested in activities, she solved her problem. Ann has always been a good kid. She keeps out of arguments and is kept content by art. The other three? Sometimes, I just don't know. When should we be arriving in Orlando?"

"In less than an hour. Back to your kids. I think you would have an extremely boring summer if they were all angels. Janie seeks too much attention. Doesn't she?"

"I know. She's unhappy. I'm very anxious to meet her parents. I'm hoping that it might give me a clue as to what is disturbing her."

"One lesson I learned in my psychology course is that kids, like Janie, can be hungry for attention because they only receive criticism instead of praise. At the same time, another family member receives approval constantly. I think the compliments she received, from being in the shows, may help straighten her out. How's Lynn?"

"Lynn has recovered physically. However, she still has problems."

"What do you mean?" Jerry asked.

"She has been spending a lot of time by herself lately," Susan continued. "Oh, I guess she wants to make friends, but Micky is still apprehensive about Lynn's intentions. The others ignore her instead of asking her to join in their activities. They act as if she wasn't around."

"That's rough when you try to make friends but are ignored. In my cabin, the boys get along well. They have their little knock-down fights occasionally. That's normal for nine-year-old boys. However, that's enough shop talk for now. After all, counselors aren't expected to talk about campers, all the time, during their day off."

After they had traveled for some distance, Jerry offered, "We should be in Orlando soon. Have you ever been there?"

"I lived there from the time I was four years old until I was six. We moved there from New York City where I was born. I really don't remember Orlando that well. What's it like?"

"Since I haven't been there often recently, my description may be a little hazy. You'll see a lot of lakes scattered throughout the city adding to its beauty. I would guess it has become much more spread out since you lived there."

"I think I remember the lakes now. I have a vague memory of my dad taking me fishing when I was little. I still love to go fishing," Susan announced.

"No kidding. I didn't know that. How would you like to go with me sometime? I know where we can get a boat and some rods. Next to swimming, I think fishing is the sport I like best."

"I'd like that."

"Fine. How about next Monday?"

"I'll let you know later during the week. Visitors Day is this coming Sunday. Will we be allowed off on Monday?"

"The only time we are not allowed off," Jerry pointed out, "is during the last week. What does Visitors Day have to do with our going somewhere?"

"I'm not familiar with Camp Floridian's rules concerning Visitors Day. Besides, Donna was very homesick during her first week of camp. I'm not sure how seeing her parents will affect her. I may need to give her special attention on Monday." Suddenly, she noticed they were approaching a large city and asked, "Is this Orlando?"

"Yes," mumbled Jerry, slowly shaking his head and wondering what it would take for Susan to stop worrying so much about her charges. It seemed ridiculous to refuse a date because one of her campers might become homesick again after Visitors Day. He was beginning to get tired of her attitude in regards to her job.

"Susan," he said deliberately. "I've been a counselor for several years. Most children get homesick for a few hours after their parents leave on Visitors Day. Some children even want to go home with their parents. Others are not concerned when their parents leave. However, homesickness is something that you have to expect. I think it would be silly for you not to take advantage of your day off. Here is some friendly advice. If you don't want to go out on Monday, I think you ought to exchange your day off with another counselor."

"You do sound like a big brother concerned about his sister's welfare; except, I don't appreciate your advice. Please, don't say anything more about this subject. Where can I get candy and comics for my girls?"

"There should be a discount store on one of these streets," he added. "Oh, Susan, can't you understand that I care for you and don't want to see you work so hard? Are you trying to become a workaholic or martyr? Because if you are, you are close to succeeding, and I would suggest you stop. I mean your attitude is really dumb. If nothing else, you are a glutton for punishment."

This infuriated Susan, and she glared at him without saying a word. Jerry found a shopping center with a five-and-dime store and parked his car. Without waiting for him to open the door, Susan quickly got out and slammed the door shut. She started marching toward the store's entrance.

"Hey, wait a minute. I need to buy something, too," he called out, as he hurried to catch up with her.

"I'm sorry, Susan," he said, when she rudely brushed past him. "I simply don't want you to take your work so seriously. Please, don't be angry."

"Jerry, do you mind," she huffed, turning back to face him. "Do you realize you can't manage my life? How I function, as a counselor, happens to be my business. Not yours. If you can't understand," she continued, "our friendship is threatened."

They entered the store, and Susan asked a sales girl where she could find comics and candy. She tried to hurry away from Jerry.

However, he refused to be brushed aside. He thought to himself, "I wish she'd be sensible" and continued to follow her around.

"Miss," he said to Susan, after she had completed her purchases. "My name is Jerry Martin. May I give you a lift? I'm going your way."

Susan nodded dumbly. They returned to the convertible, settled into the car, and started the long drive back to camp. As they rode, she sat gazing straight ahead, oblivious to all around her. She was still furious with Jerry for meddling in her affairs. Yet, perhaps, what he had said made sense. Still, she was hurt and frustrated because of him. Because of herself. She wasn't sure.

Her eyes filled with tears as Jerry drove on, and she tried to hold them back. At last, a little pool of salty tears fell from her eyes, and she wiped them away with her hand. Jerry took out his handkerchief and silently offered it to her. He drove on, as tension continued to envelop the car's occupants. What Jerry had tried to convey to Susan wasn't new to her. He had expressed it more strongly, more clearly, and, yes, more painfully, than ever before.

At last, the silence broke. "Jerry, I'm sorry. I must have seemed very silly back there. I acted like one of the children I'm supposed to be taking care of in camp. You're right, as usual, on this. I'm sorry," she repeated. She moved closer to him.

"Susan, you don't have to apologize. I had it coming. Let's forget it. O.K.?" He turned on some music then quickly turned it off as the air had not completely cleared.

They continued to ride in silence until they arrived at camp. Jerry parked his car and took their belongings out of the trunk. He handed the swimsuit and hat to Susan and walked her to the rec hall, without saying a word.

Totally miserable, Susan looked at the ground and muttered, "Thanks for lunch and for the trip to Orlando." She managed to add slowly, "It hurt, but thanks also for making me see the truth. Maybe, one of these days, I'll change." Jerry leaned over and kissed her lightly before walking away.

It was dinner time at camp. Susan wasn't hungry and decided not to join her campers at the table. She trudged back to her cabin and lay down with her head cradled between her arms.

She didn't realize her girls had returned from dinner until she heard Ann tell the others, "Hey, Susan's lying down. Let's be quiet in case she's sleeping."

Susan hastily sat up and looked at her girls as they entered the cabin door. "Hi, I bought the comics and candy you wanted." She reached into a paper bag and gave her campers their goodies.

"Susan," asked Micky, observing her counselor's red eyes, "what's wrong? Were you crying because of Jerry?"

"Of course not. Nothing's wrong," snapped Susan. "Why should I be crying because of Jerry? Now what did you do all day, girls?"

Micky was not about to be swayed from asking questions. "How come you're back so early?" she asked. She remembered the last time Susan had not returned from her date until 8:00 p.m., and most counselors didn't get back until nine or later in the evening.

"Micky, stop trying to be a detective," Susan hissed.

She proceeded to question the girls as to their activities and learned they had been taught to build a campfire. Her campers had learned various campcraft skills and were thoroughly prepared for tomorrow's campout.

Later, the campers went to the evening activity. A week ago, it had been the talent show. Tonight, no special program was arranged. They sang old favorites, in addition to the usual camp songs, and learned a few new tunes as well. Susan didn't feel like singing; instead, she headed over to the lodge or what the counselors nicknamed "their refuge."

Sometime later, as she read her new book, she heard a few counselors enter and realized one was Marla. She prepared to ignore any cutting remarks Marla might make about today's date with Jerry, and she braced herself when Marla sat next to her.

"Hi. Did you have fun with Jerry today?" Marla inquired.

"Of course. Why shouldn't I?" Susan answered coldly.

"You missed some important news concerning the counselors," Marla added in her most sarcastic tone. "You are interested in the counselor's world. Aren't you?"

Susan didn't understand what the question meant. Was Marla implying that Susan wasn't a capable counselor? Was she hinting Susan cared only about her campers? Susan wasn't sure.

"Well, anyhow, Red is leaving Camp Floridian. It seems he has to return to his ranch unexpectedly. I thought you might be interested."

"What will they do about a riding counselor?" Susan was curious. Riding was Lynn's and Micky's favorite activity. They rode every day that the camp offered it. They usually battled over which one would ride Sprinter, the little black horse they had both fallen in love with during their first day at camp.

"Don't you know anything about how camps are run?" Marla sneered. " Naturally, Mrs. Warren will hire someone else to take Red's place. In fact, I hear she has already hired one of his friends.

He's supposed to be a real hunk with a great personality. He's the type of guy I think you would like. He should be at camp in about two days. Red will stay on until he arrives."

"Oh," replied Susan, "that's very interesting." She stifled a yawn and returned to her reading.

Marla was not discouraged. "Susan, I believe in being fair. You know that. I'm much more concerned with others than I am about myself. For example, if I continue working with your girls, they will learn to shoot properly. I could loaf the entire period, couldn't I, and let them do as they pleased. You and I know that it wouldn't be fair to them."

"Sure," considered Susan silently. "No, you're not very self-centered. Nothing like that. You wouldn't dream of looking out for yourself, Marla."

"Get to the point, Marla. I'm reading an interesting book," she grumbled.

"This new counselor sounds ideal for you. I have to admit Jerry is nice. But, let's face it, he's not right for you. Now deep inside, I think you know it. Jerry is twenty-three years old. How old are you? Seventeen?"

"I happen to be nineteen and think Jerry is perfect for me. What business is it of yours anyhow?"

"Hang on. I hear the new riding counselor is twenty. He'd be a lot closer to your age, and he wouldn't be so sophisticated and hard to handle. Don't you think it would be better if you dated him? I'll even arrange it for you when he arrives. Think it over, Susan. I'm only looking out for your welfare."

"Give me a break, Marla. I like Jerry and he happens to like me. You're wasting your time trying to sell me on any new counselor.

I'm not giving up Jerry without a fight, and I don't think he wants to be given up. If this new guy is such a catch, why don't you go fishing after him?" She added dryly, "With your irresistible charm, I know he'll fall in love with you immediately. I'm sure he'll like your honesty and sincerity."

"All right. I was only thinking of you. You're passing on quite a good thing. "

"I don't mind, and I don't care to discuss this any further."

"Sorry. From now on, I'll keep the good ones for myself. It's a shame. And I offered you such a rare deal." Marla realized she was defeated and left the lodge in a rage. She now admitted she couldn't get Jerry back regardless of what method she used.

"Who knows," Marla thought, "maybe the new counselor would be special. Jerry wasn't her speed anyway. A guy would have to be very special to be worthy of her."

It was getting late. Susan returned to her cabin feeling cross and tired. She was angry with Marla for suggesting she should exchange Jerry for some unknown quantity. Susan did not intend to give him up, at least not now, and never to Marla. Did Marla think Jerry was the type for her? If she did, she was mistaken. Now it was clear why Marla had been friendly last week. The more she thought about it, the angrier she became. Jerry was terrific. At times, he was impossible, overstepping his boundary about how she wanted to run her life. Yet, that was to get her thinking straight again. During those times, in addition to being a boyfriend, he acted like a big brother. However, she was glad Jerry had not come to the lodge tonight. She was sorry about what had happened today and more critical of herself than of him.

She undressed rapidly, not caring how she flung her clothes into her cubbyholes. Tears from frustration and bitter resentment started to pour from her eyes. She threw herself on the bed and cried herself to sleep.

Chapter Eleven

The Campout

The morning sun poured through the windows of Bunk 6 with the blaring call of Reveille harshly awakening campers and counselor. "Up, everyone. This is it. Big day ahead," Susan announced.

Some of Susan's girls leisurely threw off the covers and sat up. Others lay there wanting to savor the coolness of their sheets and pillows. After several minutes, Susan prodded her girls again, "Come on, girls, you only have fifteen more minutes before line-up. Let's go, slow pokes."

This warning stirred them to action. They jumped out of their beds and rushed over to their cubby holes for their clothes.

"Susan, why didn't you tell us to hurry up?" demanded Micky.

"Is it necessary for me to come by each bed and push you out? You girls should know by now when Reveille blows, you have a half hour to get dressed. Just be thankful that you don't have to put on makeup like the older girls. Then you would have a problem."

"But," protested Donna, "reveille sometimes can't be heard if you're tired and sleeping soundly."

"That's why I call out to you. In fact, if you are still sleeping, I come over to your bed and awaken you. Maybe you should get dressed as soon as you hear the bugle, before I have a chance to remind you. Then you'll have plenty of time."

As the girls combed their hair, the whistle for lineup blew. "Let's go, girls, now," commanded Susan, hustling them out of the cabin.

Mitzi handled the roll call and seemed satisfied everyone was on time for a change. Sometimes one of the older girls came running out of her cabin, at the last moment, waving a comb to finish styling her hair. This was met by a reprimand from Mitzi either to the girl or to her counselor.

"Good morning," Mitzi said. "Today, I want everyone to have their cabins in perfect order for inspection. Some of you girls, particularly you fourteen and fifteen-year-olds, haven't been neat enough. I'm sure if the younger campers can have a clean cabin, you older ones can do it as well. Susan and Janice, a reminder: your girls are leaving on an overnight today. I guess that's all for now."

The girls wandered over to the mess hall and stood while Bunk 7 girls said grace. They quietly sat on benches. Today's menu was pancakes, a welcome change from the usual eggs or cereal. The girls, however, seemed indifferent, including Donna, who picked at her food.

"What's wrong, Donna?" Susan asked.

"Nothing," she paused. "I wonder why they can't have chocolate or berry pancakes instead of these plain ones."

"Come on, Donna, you're not at home. Remember, this is camp, not a pancake house. Put some sugar or syrup on them if you want to use something sweet," Susan answered.

"Don't worry, Donna," commented Micky. "Right before Visitors Day, we start getting real food."

Susan laughed and asked, "Does anyone have any questions about today's campout? I notice you have all been quiet this morning."

"I do," said Janie. "Will we toast marshmallows tonight?"

"Of course, silly," retorted Micky. "They always toast marshmallows at campouts. Sometimes we have s'mores. Isn't that right, Susan?"

"What's a s'more," interrupted Lynn, "I've never heard of those before."

"Sure. That's part of the fun," smiled Susan. "A s'more, Lynn, is when you put a marshmallow and two pieces of a chocolate bar in between two graham crackers. It's gooey but delicious. Now come on. Let's hurry so we can get back for cleanup."

"I still don't think I want to go tonight," grumbled Janie.

"Why not? You'll be the only one staying back," announced Micky. "Come on, Janie. I went on a campout last year. It was lots of fun."

"Because I would rather sleep on a bed," replied Janie.

"Me, too," mumbled Ann.

"Girls, we can discuss this later. Let's go. We're one of the last groups in the mess hall." Her campers rose from the table and lazily returned to the cabin. After prodding by Susan, they straightened their cubby holes and started on their chores.

Her charges, except for Micky, continued to work silently, moping around as if they had the world's weight on their shoulders. Eventually, Lynn spoke up, "Susan, I've never been on a campout before. What's it like?"

"Is that why you're so unhappy today? Are some of you worried about roughing it? I don't think you should feel uneasy about it. Camping in the woods is fun. Haven't you ever wanted to sleep in a tent or go on an adventure? Micky, you said you went last year. Did you enjoy yourself?"

"Yes, I did, and I want to go this year, too. Come on, everyone, where we camp is great. It's a clearing surrounded by pines, and you can look up and see the stars. I think you'll like it. I felt about campouts like you do this year. I didn't want to go, but after I was there, I had a great time."

Susan addressed her girls again. "Are you worried about whether you will have fun or not? Is that the problem?"

Ann and Donna nodded their heads. Finally Lynn muttered, "I'm not sure whether I want to go either."

"I guess it would be nice to get out of camp. What about wild animals?" pointed out Janie.

"Relax. The wildest animals around here are, perhaps, a few deer and squirrels," Susan assured them. She looked at her watch. "Oh! Oh! We have about ten more minutes to inspection. You think about what we've discussed, and I'm sure you'll change your minds."

They continued to clean the cabin. At about a quarter to nine, Mitzi strode through the door calling out, "Is everyone ready? Time for inspection." The girls had just finished their work and nodded. "Well, let's see. Your beds and cubby holes are fine."

She went into the bathroom. "Someone didn't let all the water out of the basin. It looks a little messy. Whose job was that?"

"Mine," answered Lynn, hesitantly.

"Lynn, use the sponge more thoroughly from now on. Otherwise, your cabin is fine. See you tomorrow."

Mitzi left, and Micky yelled at Lynn, "Don't you care if we ever get a ten? Thanks, Lynn. I'm sure everyone else appreciates it."

"I'm sorry. I tried to do my best," Lynn mumbled.

"Why don't you stop trying and just do your best," cracked Micky as she stormed out of the cabin

"Micky," Susan called, following her. "Since when do you have the authority to speak to Lynn like that? It seems to me, you don't always do your job perfectly either. Now go apologize."

"Why?" asked Micky, shrugging her shoulders defiantly.

"I told you why. Trying hard is what counts, not perfection. Now go inside and tell Lynn you're sorry."

Micky glared at Susan, stuck both hands into her pants' pockets, and stomped into the cabin. She turned to Lynn. "I'm sorry, but you deserved it," she grunted, after she realized Susan meant business.

The campers went to their usual Tuesday morning activities of nature and arts and crafts. Although they still expected to go on their campout and hike to the site, they would not leave until after their rest hour. At arts and crafts, Jean welcomed them and told them they would be working again on ceramics. She showed them molds of cups and plates. Campers could make either one since the entire period would be spent on creating the crockery of their choice.

Surprisingly, all the girls decided to make cups. Their enthusiasm seemed to burst forth, once more, as they actively participated in the class. Jean gave general instructions before assisting here and there. The campers worked well on this project. At the period's end, they had completed painting the cups and were ready to glaze their pieces in a kiln.

Following crafts, the girls strode over to the nature building discussing what they would do with their cups. Donna wanted to make two, one for each parent.

Barbara, the nature counselor, greeted them pleasantly. "I hear you are going on a campout tonight. They're loads of fun. You can see nature first hand and enjoy it better when you rough it. Are you anxious to go?"

"I am," shouted Micky. The rest of the girls did not reply since they remained undecided.

"Today, I thought we would do something different," Barbara continued, "As you know, we usually talk about an animal or a plant. Today, we'll talk about the stars. Tonight, you'll have a good opportunity to practice what you learn in today's class. First, have you seen our new addition? One of the boys brought in a garter snake to our nature hut. It's right over there." The girls strolled over to examine it.

"What does it eat?" asked Donna.

"Frogs and fish as well as cold blooded animals."

"Is he poisonous?" inquired Lynn, remembering her experience.

"No, they're harmless. Garter snakes live in every state as well as in Canada, Mexico, and Central America. Any more questions?" The girls shook their heads.

"Fine. Let's talk about what you'll see tonight...the stars. I'll teach you about constellations and how to recognize them. I'm sure Susan will point them out to you. As you know, many, many stars form our galaxy, the Milky Way. Who knows what a constellation is?"

"I do," shouted Micky. "It's a collection of stars."

"That's right," agreed Barbara.

She continued, until the period's end, telling them about Orion, the Big Dipper, and other constellations they might recognize. At last, the period ended. Enthusiasm seemed, once more, to engulf the entire group. It would be fun to sleep under the stars and try to recognize different formations.

As they walked back toward the cabin to change for general swim, Susan turned to them again, "Well, girls, have you decided? Do you want to go?"

All of them answered "yes" except Janie.

"Come on, Janie. It will be great. We can recognize the stars and eat food out-of-doors. I can smell those hot dogs now," breathed Lynn.

"I don't know," she whined. "I guess I'll go." Janie was not very enthusiastic.

"Good. Well, that's settled. I know you will all have a good time. Now off to general swim." There was no need to repeat herself as her girls went dashing to the cabin to change into their bathing suits. Susan wondered what had happened to her campers. During the morning, they had been sullen and uncooperative. Now, they acted as if everything was all right. Maybe they had just needed an incentive such as star gazing at the overnight. Oh, well, she was due for lifeguard duty during the swim. She had better hurry and catch up with her group.

The swimming area was divided into two sections, one for the boys and one for the girls. Wooden docks, called cribs, shaped like huge letter E's placed back to back, surrounded the sections. A little farther out, past the cribs, advanced swimmers had floating rafts. While campers swam, counselors stood on the long side of the E's with bamboo poles anticipating any emergencies.

General swim was uneventful. During the middle of the period, a whistle blew for the campers to come ashore so counselors could have their turn. As soon as the campers waded onto the beach, Susan made a graceful dive into the advanced swimming area.

Jerry swam over to her and observed, "Isn't the water great today?"

"It sure is," admitted Susan. Being no longer angry, she was now content to have him join her.

"We have just enough time for me to challenge you to a race to the raft. How about it?" he suggested.

"Sure. But I want a five-second lead," insisted Susan.

They climbed back on the crib and dove off the docks with Jerry giving Susan a head start. Even with her receiving this advantage, it wasn't much of a race. Susan's shorter, choppier strokes could not keep up with Jerry's longer, smoother strokes, and he easily won. After he had clambered onto the raft, he gave her a hand and pulled her up beside him. Just then the whistle blew, signaling for counselors to come out of the water. The two had little opportunity for conversation and hurriedly swam back to the docks to resume their posts.

"Good race, Jerry," Susan called to him.

"It was. See you after general swim," he answered with a broad grin, as he left for the other side of the two E's. The rest of the period seemed to go slowly. At last, it was over. Everyone scrambled for towels and beach shoes.

Jerry walked over to Susan and asked, "Will I see you later this afternoon? How about tonight? I'm not on OD."

"Jerry, I have to take my girls on an overnight today so, unfortunately, I won't be able to see you later." She looked over at her campers. "I see my girls are ready to return to the cabin. See you tomorrow though."

"Fine. Tomorrow it is," mumbled Jerry, slowly walking toward the waterfront shack.

Lunch consisted of macaroni and cheese highlighted by everyone receiving a piece of chocolate cake for dessert. Bunk 6 seemed more enthusiastic to go on a campout. They devoured their meal and walked quickly back to their cabin. They organized their camping gear instead of lying down during rest hour. No one, except Micky, had brought their own sleeping bags to camp. They had, instead, borrowed this equipment from girls in the other cabins.

After they packed flashlights, canteens, blankets, and extra clothing in their sleeping bag rolls, they followed Susan to the mess hall and infirmary to get the supplies they needed. She managed to obtain coolers loaded with hot dogs, bacon, and eggs, as well as thermos bottles of water and lemonade. In addition, she assembled large stacks of paper plates and cups and all the other food and equipment they would require. They returned immediately to the cabin.

At last, rest hour ended. Bunk 6 changed into jeans and carried their sweaters. Soon they would be joined by Bunk 7, another cabin group of approximately the same age.

"Are you ready, girls?" Susan inquired.

"Yes," they shouted.

"Well, all right, let's go," Susan commanded. "Let's see if Bunk 7 is ready."

They traipsed over to Bunk 7, carrying all the supplies, and learned everything was set. Shortly afterwards, the two groups of girls started hiking down the road to the camp site, a mile and a half away.

Bunk 7's counselor was Janice Myers, another general counselor. This was her third year as a counselor at Camp Floridian, and she knew all the routines connected with campouts. She was an attractive girl: blonde, tall, and lean, and quite popular with the male counselors.

Her cabin group consisted of a few ten-year-olds but mostly eleven-year-olds. Since camping was more fun when two groups of the same age went together, one of Mrs. Warren's rules on overnights was that two or three cabins always went on the same trip.

As they hiked, Bunk 7 started to sing. Soon all lent their voices. It seemed to make the hike go faster, and they quickly arrived at the site. Campers spread blankets on the ground and unrolled sleeping bags. The two counselors promptly set up their equipment and led the girls in games.

"Susan," called out Janice, "why don't you appoint one of your girls to be the leader, and we'll run some relay races? We have twelve girls between us, and we can divide them into three groups. I brought some balls."

"Let me be a leader, Susan," pleaded Janie.

"That's a very good idea. All right, Janie, you can pick one of the teams." The two cabin groups played for an hour, laughing, shouting, and enjoying themselves. Afterwards, Susan led them in some quiet games such as Chain Stories and Geography.

In the middle of Geography, Micky interrupted the game. "Susan, can we play soccer instead of this?"

The girls became excited at this idea. Soon, a quiet time erupted into an active sport. The campers played well, especially Bunk 7. It appeared Susan's girls were having a better time than they had anticipated. Even Janie seemed to have fun as she was laughing and shouting with the rest.

The two counselors called the games to a halt at sunset. Since Janice was in charge of preparations for dinner, she instructed, "Before you can cook your dinner, you are each to find and bring back a long branch of dead wood. When you find one, come back here, and I'll give you a hot dog to put on it. You'll each receive two frankfurters. If you have trouble finding a sturdy stick, call me, and I'll help you. Susan, will you please prepare the baked beans and get ready to give out the hot dog rolls. We'll have dinner as soon as everything is ready."

The girls searched in different directions. Most found branches without too much difficulty.

"Janice," shouted Donna, "I can't find any."

"Just a second, Donna," she answered. "Susan, why don't you pass out the lemonade while I help Donna." She marched over to the camper. They searched until they had found a suitable stick.

"By the way, girls," Janice continued, "I brought chocolate bars, graham crackers, and marshmallows in case you want to have s'mores." Great enthusiasm from the campers answered this announcement as the campers of Bunk 6 and 7 eagerly awaited this special treat.

Some campers had already bent down to roast their hot dogs over the open fire they had built. Others impatiently waited for their turn. Finally, everyone had cooked their dinner, and the two cabin groups sat eating.

Susan placed a huge log on the blaze encouraging the blue and orange flames of the fire to a more majestic height. The fire had the pungent odor characteristic of burning firewood. The group looked contented, some still eating their dinners, and some now roasting marshmallows. Many toasted marshmallows were a burnt black. They gave off a little flame of their own when campers lifted them from the fire. All of the girls then approached Janice for the supplies needed to make s'mores.

After the sky darkened, the children's faces lit up from the fire as they watched the flames. Sitting on their blankets, the girls softly sang familiar songs. Their counselors looked at them proudly and smiled at each other knowingly. It was a beautiful night. The stars shone brightly with a full moon in view. Trees surrounded the group, their branches reaching to the sky, dancing to and fro in the path of the south wind.

It was getting late. The campers of Bunks 6 and 7 tried to identify the constellations about which they had learned. Susan pointed to different groups of stars and identified them by name. It was a clear night. Perfect for an overnight.

At last, Susan and Janice told their campers to prepare for bed. The girls crawled into their sleeping bags and soon fell asleep. Before Janie closed her eyes, she cried out for Susan, who came to her side.

"What is it, Janie? Can't you sleep?"

The child nodded her head and said quietly, "Susan, I'm glad I came."

Her counselor leaned over and tenderly brushed Janie's hair off of her forehead. "I'm glad, too, Janie. This has been fun. Good night."

The counselors discussed the evening's activities, made plans for breakfast tomorrow, and brought the fire's flames under control. They placed rocks around the fire as a safety measure before crawling into their sleeping bags. It was easy to fall asleep amidst the hooting of the night owls and the rustling of leaves as a soft breeze flowed through them. The sounds of night filled the air along with the gentle breathing of the girls.

In the early morning, Susan called to the girls so they could see the sunrise. Micky had asked Susan to awaken them, the night before, and the others had eagerly agreed. Ann was already up, poised with a camera to take a snapshot of the sunrise so she could paint a picture of it later.

However, Susan had a difficult time getting the rest of her campers up. "What's the big idea? It's still dark out," complained Lynn. She cradled her head between her arms and closed her eyes.

Susan attempted once more to awaken her with a gentle shove and said, "Come on, Lynn, wake up. Don't you want to see the sunrise? It will be beautiful."

"Oh, sure," yawned Lynn, sitting up and rubbing her eyes, heavy with fatigue.

Susan aroused Donna and Janie. Though sleepy, they managed to sit up when Susan promised them they could return to bed as soon as they reached their cabin. Micky and the girls in Bunk 7, however, protested loudly. However, after much prodding, they stirred and lazily sat up in their sleeping bags.

Breathtaking colors appeared in the east, which held everyone's attention. It was much more exciting than watching a sunset. For most of the girls, seeing a sunrise was rare.

Susan thought to herself, "The best times to enjoy a sunrise are either at a campout or when one is on water in a boat, with a fishing rod in hand, waiting for a nibble." Susan had seen the sunrise on both occasions and felt it was one of nature's wonders.

Later that morning, the campers thanked Susan for having awakened them in time to see the sunrise. Ann, especially, had been delighted to see it.

"Well," snickered Micky, "I guess Ann won't be saying I want to paint the sunset anymore. Now, she'll say, 'I want to paint the sunrise.' Right, Ann?"

The others in Bunk 6 laughed while Ann blushed. "Why can't the rest of you enjoy nature as much as I do?" she wondered.

"It's beautiful. I love nature," she emphatically asserted.

"How about breakfast, kids?" Janice interrupted. She had finished frying eggs over the fire built to last night's height. The campers greedily gathered around, pushing their paper plates in her face.

"Hold on there! Stop that! Bunk 7, you wait until I've served Susan's girls," she ordered. Her campers protested.

Janice repeated, "I mean it. Sit down now. We have enough for everyone. I'm only serving after you sit down."

Resentfully, they returned to their blankets while Susan and Janice served the food. They became indignant because they felt it was unfair for another cabin group to be served before them. The eggs and the accompanying hot chocolate were delicious. The girls enjoyed this type of breakfast much more on a campout than at the mess hall. The smoke seemed to enhance the flavor.

Bunk 6 socialized with Janice's girls talking about camp and their hobbies. Some campers even brought boys into the conversation. They had reached the stage where they had stopped thinking boys were silly human beings. Some of the ten-year-olds, to the amazement of others, admitted they liked being with boys. All the eleven-year-olds were eager to spend time with boys.

At 10:00 a.m., after everyone had finished breakfast, Susan called out, "It's time to start walking back to camp. When you get back to your cabins, shake out your blankets and put your clothes and equipment away."

The comments of several campers interrupted her. "What does she think we are? Babies?" "We know what to do."

Lynn complained, "Susan, don't you think we know camp routine? After all, this is our fifth week."

"Girls," said Janice, "I think we have to tell you what and what not to do. Speaking for my campers, I know it would be a mistake to have inspection during the middle of the day. We would probably get about a four."

"Did you have fun?" inquired Susan. Greeted by a chorus of "yes," she was delighted.

It was a chance to get away from camp and eat food cooked over a fire, to see the sunrise, and to enjoy a break in the usual routine. The group, tired from the experience, walked toward camp silently. After they took their hot showers, they could look forward to resting on their beds where they could relax for as long as they desired. They would not have to report for lunch. One girl started humming a tune, and some of the others joined in. Singing at camp was contagious. At last, they walked through the camp gate and started singing, "We're Here Because We're Here," a camp song always sung upon the return to camp from a trip, a hike, or a campout.

The two groups wandered over to their cabins. Instead of following Susan's instructions, they crawled onto their beds and slept, tired but happy.

Chapter Twelve

Waiting for Visitors Day

The girls continued to talk about how much fun the overnight had been. However, another topic soon entered into their conversation. This coming Sunday, in only three more days, the campers would see their families. Visitors Day would be here at last. They frequently received letters from parents, relatives, and friends. However, that wasn't the same as being with loved ones, face to face.

Reveille announced Friday morning's arrival. Susan did not have to remind her girls to hurry and get dressed since they had learned that lesson on Tuesday. Still, it seemed the whistle blew much too soon for lineup. Bunk 6 had to rush to be at the flag pole on time.

This morning, after Mitzi completed roll call, Susan's girls had the honor of raising the flag. Each of her girls begged Susan for the privilege and eagerly waved their hands in her face. She finally appointed Donna and Ann. The two proudly marched to the flag pole where Mitzi gave them the banner. Accompanied by the singing of "God Bless America" by the entire girls' division, they slowly hoisted the flag up the pole. Mitzi read announcements, and the girls left for breakfast.

The entire camp waited impatiently outside the mess hall until the doors opened, and then they noisily dashed to their tables. After the customary blessing, campers and counselors eagerly sat for breakfast. Susan's girls thought the food didn't taste quite as good as at the campout. However, they stuffed themselves anyway.

"I can't wait until Sunday. I sure hope it hurries and gets here," announced Ann.

"Me, too. Days don't go fast when you want them to, Ann, but they shouldn't go slowly either. It's not fair," protested Donna.

"Girls, are all your families coming?" Susan inquired.

She looked forward to meeting the other parents and wondered what they would be like. Mrs. Kingston, Lynn's mother, she remembered, was difficult. She was glad Mr. Kingston had been so understanding when the snake bit Lynn. He had calmed his wife, who might have caused considerable trouble for Susan and the camp. Lynn had stopped being so sarcastic and irritable since she had seen her mother and father. Susan wondered how the other girls would react to seeing their families.

"My parents won't be here," muttered Lynn. "They went to Europe. Remember, Susan."

"You mean your mom and dad won't see you until the end of camp. Gee, I'm glad mine aren't like that," observed Micky. "I can hardly wait until they're here."

"Don't forget, Micky, Lynn was lucky. She saw her parents a couple of weeks ago when we didn't see ours. So that isn't so bad," added Donna.

Ann interrupted, "No sense being alone, Lynn. If you want to, you can spend the day with my mother and me. She's an artist and a terrific person."

Lynn shook her head, "Thanks anyway, Ann. I would rather be by myself."

Susan quickly spoke up. "No way, Lynn. Since your parents aren't coming, you'll spend Visitors Day with me. After I meet everyone's families, we'll do something special together. How about it? I don't want you to be alone."

Lynn glanced at Susan and shrugged.

Bunk 6 discussed where they planned to take their parents on Visitors Day. Ann was determined to show her mother the arts and crafts building. The others agreed. They also looked forward to taking theirs to the lake and stables. The water show, which the camp planned for Sunday, also crept into their conversation.

For the past week, during optional swim, twelve campers had been rehearsing a water ballet to be presented on Visitors Day. They performed expertly at rehearsals, and the swimming counselors were especially enthusiastic. In addition, the camp would hold races with both beginning swimmers and those more advanced participating. Jack, the water-skiing counselor, planned an exhibition by campers skilled in skiing. Lynn expected to perform in this event and in the girls' intermediate races. The rest of Bunk 6 would participate in the water contests.

During inspection, Susan's campers received a perfect score for one of the few times that summer. Noting how spotless their cabin was, Mitzi told them how pleased she was to give them a "ten." Susan informed her girls that she, too, was delighted with their work. Now, she insisted, if they could learn to keep a neat cabin throughout the day, that would be something special.

Volleyball followed the first period of arts and crafts. On the way to the field, Lynn complained, "Come on, Susan, it's too hot to play. Let's go back to the cabin."

"I agree with Lynn," sympathized Micky, "and I'm leaving for Bunk 6 now." She headed in that direction, with Lynn quickly following behind her.

"Hold on, girls. Micky and Lynn, come back here," Susan demanded. "I know it's hot, but it's impossible for you to stay in the cabin by yourselves. Everyone has to participate in activities. You know that. I'll tell you what I'll do. If Bunk 5 is willing, you only have to play for forty-five minutes instead of the usual hour. Now let's go."

Susan ushered her girls on their way after Lynn and Micky returned to the group. Grumbling and groaning, they all tagged after her. Stopping to get a volleyball at the equipment shack, they proceeded to the volleyball playing area.

They found the net placed in the middle of a field surrounded by grass that sprung up as rapidly as maintenance mowed it. Bunk 5, consisting of nine- and ten-year-olds, arrived shortly afterwards. They, too, dragged as they reached the meadow.

Volleyball started with Bunk 5 challenging Bunk 6 to three games or as many as they had time to play. To compensate for Bunk 5 having two more players than Bunk 6, Susan decided to join her group's team. Tina, Bunk 5's counselor, flipped a coin to see which team would go first. Bunk 5 won the toss and served the ball.

Campers shouted "Get it over the net," "Hit it," and "Can't you play volleyball?" Most of the campers did not know how to play well. Nevertheless, they seemed to enjoy themselves. Several campers started complaining about the high temperature, saying they could get heatstroke.

At last, Susan called, "Time" and stopped the game.

"What's wrong, Susan?" questioned Tina.

"I have to agree with the kids. It's a little too hot out here to play for sixty minutes. I don't know about your campers. When we started, mine didn't want to participate at all because of this heat." She wiped her forehead where beads of perspiration hung suspended.

"All right, people, let's call it quits for today. The final score of this game is Bunk 5- fourteen, Bunk 6-ten. Each bunk has won a game. Super!" Tina announced.

The two groups trudged back to their cabins to change into swimsuits for general swim. The water would feel cool after being in the hot sun for almost an hour. Susan looked forward to diving into the lake and, perhaps, spending a few minutes with Jerry. They hadn't seen each other since Wednesday's swim and then only for a few moments. Suddenly, she realized he was constantly in her thoughts.

At the lake, she glanced over at the boys' crib, where Jerry should have had dock duty. He was nowhere in the area. Susan spotted Mike and asked, "Have you seen Jerry?"

"I think Jerry said he was working on plans for the water show. He's making out a schedule with Jack. I don't think he'll be here this period. Any message I can give him?" he responded.

Susan shook her head. "Thanks anyway, Mike. I'll try to see him later today." She strolled over to take her post on the docks.

Soon came the campers' turn to plunge into the lake. While she watched her girls near the shore splash around like pollywogs, Susan decided she, too, would go swimming. The water looked refreshing. It was a clear blue except where campers splashed. It seemed like an eternity until it was her turn, perhaps because she was disappointed Jerry wasn't at the lake.

While swimming, her thoughts again turned to Visitors Day. Susan wondered if she would say the right thing when she met her girls' parents. What did counselors say when she was a camper? She couldn't quite remember. Oh, they greeted parents pleasantly and told them how well their child was getting along. Susan scolded herself for thinking this way as she resumed her post.

The remainder of general swim seemed to go faster. Soon her girls returned to the cabin to change for lunch. Lunches at camp consisted of cold meals such as salads or sandwiches with a hot dinner served at night.

As with all meals lately, the girls discussed their parents as they sat at their table.

"I hope my parents bring me a package. Last year, they brought me some salt water taffy and licorice. Some of my bunkmates also got packages, and we had a party. It was great," commented Micky.

"I wonder if I write a letter to my mother today, will she get it before she comes on Sunday? I could tell her to bring us some food. It would be super if we could have a party this year," said Ann.

"I don't think so, but you can try," offered Susan. "Anyone want seconds on dessert? It's very good pudding."

"I do," shouted Micky. She reached greedily across the table for the pudding, upsetting Donna's glass of milk. The milk started oozing all over Bunk 6's place settings. Susan promptly sprang into action. She grabbed all the napkins in sight and started sponging. Her girls hurriedly rose from the table, backing away as milk continued to spread. The rest of camp quickly turned their heads toward them to see what the commotion was all about.

"Micky, just don't stand there. Go get a sponge from the kitchen. Go on," Susan hollered. Micky, who had been standing dumbstruck, moved rapidly toward the kitchen doors.

"Boy, what a klutz," muttered Lynn. "Can I help, Susan?"

"Yes, help me wipe with these napkins. Mop as fast as you can."

"You would think Micky would have better manners. Lately she has been so different. She's like you used to be, Lynn, a real pain in the neck." Ann shook her head in disgust.

Janie and Donna greeted this comment with a chorus of "Yeahs" as they continued to stand back with looks of disdain.

They finally cleaned up the spilled milk, and Bunk 6 sat finishing their lunch. By this time, no one was hungry any longer. Dismissed from the dining room, they ambled back to their cabin for rest hour.

Micky, embarrassed over what had happened, walked away from the others. "I'm sorry," she whispered to Susan.

"It was an accident. However, from now on, when you want something, don't reach, ask for it. I'm sure you'll get what you want. Now don't worry, accidents happen," Susan assured her.

Quiet prevailed during rest hour. Micky and Lynn lay on their bunks while the other three played jacks. Susan, too, used the period to rest as she lay on her bed, writing to her friends back home. She wished someone would come to see her this Sunday. However, counselors could have their friends and family only on their day off, never on Visitors Day.

"Oh, well," reflected Susan, "I'll be busy. Besides, I do have Lynn to look after, and I won't have much time for myself. It's just as well."

Following rest hour, the girls left for their optional activities. Susan walked over to the lake to help teach fishing for the rest of the day. Since she was a general counselor, she worked during these periods with other counselors who needed an assistant. The exception was when Susan put out the newspaper, a class she held two afternoons each week. Then, she was her own boss.

The hours passed quickly for Susan. At the afternoon's end, though, her charges complained that, for them, it had been the slowest hours of camp. They were learning how anticipation tended to do strange things to time. Waiting for Sunday to arrive was becoming unbearable.

Dinner tasted great. For the first time that summer, it included roast beef with fresh string beans and real mashed potatoes and gravy.

"I can't believe how delicious the meal is," commented Janie. "They're not even serving instant potatoes tonight."

"That's to make a good impression on our parents," Micky explained. "You know when they ask us what we've been eating, we won't say hamburgers but instead roast beef. I heard we get barbecued chicken with french fries tomorrow."

"That's kind of sneaky, but, at least, we're getting decent food now," pointed out Janie.

"I don't think the food is bad," added Ann, "except for those eggs. They must come from a balloon factory. I think they make them out of yellow rubber."

"Now, girls, enough. Many people in this world would like those eggs and the food we eat regularly. You know we have chicken twice a week," reprimanded Susan in an authoritarian voice.

"I'll gladly give them the eggs," snickered Donna. This brought a burst of laughter from the other girls.

"I don't think that's funny," criticized Susan. "You shouldn't joke about the food." She, however, was barely able to keep a straight face herself.

"Aw, Susan, you have to admit Donna is kindhearted," gasped Lynn, as she continued to giggle away. The others thought this was also amusing. By the time they finished dinner, neither campers nor counselor could keep a straight face, no matter what they tried.

After their dismissal from the mess hall, Bunk 6 went gaily to the cabin together. This was one of the few times they had all mixed well that summer. The others had started to like Lynn more, even Micky. However, at times, Micky was still doubtful Lynn would continue to be friendly and cooperative. Lynn would have to continue to prove herself, in Micky's estimation, before they could be more than just bunkmates.

The girls played a game of catch, using tennis balls, before evening activity. All the Bunk 6 campers played. Micky and Lynn, the group's two athletes, tossed balls to each other which sailed high through the air. The others played a more conservative type of catch, lobbing the ball easily to one another, instead. At last, it was time to wander over to the rec hall for evening activity, and Susan joined her girls.

Friday night was always movie night at camp. However, tonight they would play charades since the films for this week's show had not arrived in the mail. Two cabin groups of the same age played against each other. They chose a slogan, the name of a book, or a song title from a hat. Counselors, appointed as judges, timed them to see how long it took teams to guess the answer. After three tries for each team, the group which used the least amount of time won.

Bunk 9 boys played against Bunk 8 boys. It looked like a sure victory for Bunk 9, but the younger cabin group figured out the last slogan in record time and won the contest. Then two of the older girl cabins had their chance to participate.

It was fun. The campers shouted out what they thought were the correct words as the phrase was acted out. Sometimes, it became so noisy, shouting seemed to echo off the walls. The audience joined in actively by trying to figure out what they thought was the answer and offering suggestions to teams. In about an hour, the camp directors called the evening activity to a halt and handed out ice cold watermelon to everyone. After they devoured their treats, all the campers from Bunks 1 through 6, both boys and girls, returned to their cabins.

"It's not fair," complained Donna. "We go on a campout with Bunk 7. They are less than one year older than we are. But they get to stay up later than we do."

"Yeah, we should get the same curfew," agreed Janie.

"Now, girls, a big difference exists between ten and eleven years of age," explained Susan.

Lynn interrupted her. "Some difference. One of the kids in their cabin is younger than I am. She is only ten and a half. I'll be eleven two months before her birthday. Do you think that's fair?"

"You'll get the same curfew as they do next year. Listen, girls, life is not always fair. Sometimes, it seems things are unfair. When you look at the situation carefully, you will see that's not the case, after all. For example, take a look at the CITs. They aren't much younger than the staff assistants. They're fifteen while the assistants are sixteen. The assistants have a later curfew than the CITs and also get free room and board but no salary. The CITs, on the other hand, have to pay half the camping fee and do almost as much work.

However, CITs are getting valuable experience, which will help them when they become assistants next year."

Her girls had been stomping behind her toward the cabin and reached the door. "Since you are younger, you need more rest than the older campers. Come on, stop pouting. You will, as I said before, receive the same privileges as Bunk 7 next year. Now get ready for bed."

The campers undressed slowly, petulant and resentful. It seemed to them, regardless of what Susan said, it still wasn't fair. Camp rules cheated them out of a precious half hour of activity. Susan prodded them to bed and said, "Good night."

She was on OD and took along a magazine to read while sitting on the patio. Although she didn't mind OD, no counselor actually liked it. They preferred to go to the lodge or to a nearby restaurant with another counselor or boyfriend.

After about an hour, she peered into the five cabins for which she was responsible, to make sure everything was all right. While walking around, she noticed a beautiful night as stars seemed to twinkle here and there in little groups highlighted by a golden moon which seemed to light up the entire sky.

Two hours later, her OD responsibility behind her, it became time to retire. Susan entered the cabin and prepared for bed. Her girls breathed softly in their sleep, tucked in under lightweight blankets, with some clutching their pillows. She had become very fond of them. They were all good children. She was proud and happy to be their counselor. On this train of thought, she soon drifted off to sleep.

Tensions increased Saturday in anticipation of Visitors Day. The girls continued to talk about their parents. Micky hoped her parents would bring her little sister. The day dragged painfully.

At the mess hall, after dinner, Mrs. Warren addressed the entire camp. "Boys and girls, I know how anxious you are to see your parents tomorrow. Before you go back to your cabins to change for evening activity, I want to remind you of a few things. You can see your parents as soon as inspection is over. However, before Mitzi and Ted can allow you to go to the gate, your cabin must be spotless. That means the sooner you get your work done properly, the sooner you can be dismissed. So, everyone, I want you to work hard.

"Next, I want you to wear your camp uniforms of blue shorts and white Camp Floridian T-shirts. That way we'll look like a well-dressed camp. Here is your schedule for tomorrow. Your parents can go anywhere on campus until after lunch. Lunch is at noon, and you can eat with your families. After lunch, all campers and counselors must return to their cabins for rest hour. There will be no exceptions."

A chorus of "Boo's" and "That's not fair's" from the campers met this.

Mrs. Warren held up her hand to get their attention, before continuing, "Sorry, everyone. Rules are rules. We will have our water show right after rest hour so your parents can see you swim. Finally, your parents can stay until after dinner as we'll be serving a box supper. At 6:00 p.m., though, all families must leave. I hope you have a wonderful time tomorrow, and I'm sure you will. See you at tonight's movies."

The campers piled out of the rec hall with many grumbling to themselves. A camp shouldn't have so many dumb rules. It didn't seem fair to be told what to do when, supposedly, they had a day of fun with their families.

Mrs. Warren had also mailed these same instructions to all the parents. Visitors Day was the camp's highlight for them and their children. You didn't realize how much you loved your family until you lived away from them for a while.

Bunk 6 complained endlessly about how time crawled. The movies had finally started, which included several cartoons. Her girls weren't very interested in watching. They asked Susan frequently what time it was and remained disappointed when told it was only fifteen or twenty minutes later.

As her five campers prepared for bed, Donna turned to Susan. "Why does time go so slowly when you want it to go so fast?"

"Yeah," added Micky, "I can't wait to see my parents. Last year it seemed the days crept by before Visitors Day and then the hours flew by while I was with them. Time is crazy."

"Girls, I can't explain it. I've often been puzzled by that question myself. Time can go slowly or very fast depending on the situation. However, sometimes time moves just right. Now, if you'll go to bed, morning will soon be here. How about going to sleep?"

"Aw, Susan, that's no answer," said a disappointed Donna.

"Well, that's the way it is," Susan answered with finality. She waited until all her campers went to bed and turned out the light. "Good night," she called closing the screen door behind her.

Chapter Thirteen

Visitors Day

Early Sunday morning, the sun's rays burst through the cabin's jalousie windows. The sunshine spread cheer as if forecasting today would be a special one for the campers. Reveille blasted loud and clear, and the girls promptly sat up in bed. They looked at each other and smiled.

Micky exclaimed, "Visitors Day is here at last. Susan, you were right. The night does make time pass quickly."

"How much longer do we have to wait until they allow our parents inside Camp Floridian's pearly gates?" whined Janie.

Susan looked at her watch and saw it was only 7:30. "Sorry, girls, since your parents aren't allowed to see you until 10:00 a.m., you have two and a half hours to go."

"Last year, some parents didn't get here until noon," observed Micky. "My mother and father thought parents weren't allowed to come to camp before eleven. They thought they were early when they arrived at a quarter to eleven. Boy, was I upset. You know what? When I was with them, I wasn't unhappy anymore."

The girls had been lying around on their beds and were beginning to get up. Hoping to coax them, Susan announced, "Come on, everyone. I would suggest you get ready while you're talking. Lineup is in twenty minutes. I don't want to push you out of the cabin like I did on Friday."

"Remember," she added, "the more you do, the quicker the time goes."

The girls decided to follow Susan's advice and left their beds. The campers of Bunk 6 appreciated any activity which made the hours pass more speedily, even getting dressed.

"I hope my parents are on time. It seems like an eternity since I saw them last," complained Donna.

Susan smiled and said she understood. She had gone through the same feelings when she was a camper. Perhaps, it was these experiences that helped make Susan an excellent counselor.

The whistle for lineup broke the silence, and the girls, dressed in their camp uniforms, streamed out of the cabins. They wore spotless outfits since everyone wanted to make a good impression. They looked like an army regiment ready for a dress parade.

"I'm pleased all of you remembered to wear your camp uniform today. You look great," Mitzi addressed them after roll call. She continued, "Girls, you can take your parents anywhere on campus except certain places that are off limits such as the cabins during rest hour or when you change for your swim. I want to add one more thought. Have a great time today. I'm sure you will."

She dismissed them, and they headed for the mess hall. As they waited outside the building, Donna asked impatiently, "Susan, what time is it now?"

"It's 7:45, Donna. Relax. It's only fifteen minutes later than the last time you asked."

As the mess hall doors opened, Bunk 6 strolled over to their table. This morning, breakfast looked appetizing. Large platters of bacon and waffles lined the tables as well as gallon jugs of milk.

"Camp Floridian must be trying very hard to make a good impression," observed Lynn. She sighed, "I wish my parents were coming today."

"Lynn, my offer still goes. If you want to join my mother and me, you can. Won't you change your mind?" consoled Ann.

"No, thanks, Ann. I'm going to read a book," sulked Lynn. She wanted to join Ann, but her pride would not allow her. She didn't want to depend on others for company.

"Oh, well, maybe you'll change your mind later," Ann smiled. "Breakfast is great today. They ought to have Visitors Day more often."

Conversation at the breakfast table focused again on where they would take their parents. "I want to take mine to the stables to see Sprinter. I love that horse!" exclaimed Micky excitedly.

"Not me," declared Donna. "I want to take my parents to the lake and the nature hut. I can picture my mother when she sees the garter snake." She laughed out loud as the image formed in her mind.

"I'm going to give my parents a complete guided tour around camp. They aren't interested in my activities," pouted Janie.

"I'm sure they are," soothed Susan.

Janie interrupted her. "Oh, no, they aren't. All they care about is my brother, Don, because he is an all 'A' student and president of his high school class. They don't care about me, at all."

Susan decided not to argue with the child. She thought, "Perhaps this is what is troubling Janie. Does she feel neglected? How can any parent care a great deal more about one child than another? Janie must be mistaken."

"Ann, where are you taking your parents?" asked Susan.

Ann looked at her counselor. Susan could see pain in her facial expression and in her eyes. "Only my mother is coming. I lost my dad to cancer this spring."

Susan was taken back. Of course, she should have recalled that. What a stupid mistake. She had been told all the family facts about her children. This should not have slipped her mind. "I'm sorry, Ann," the counselor said softly. "I remember now."

Suddenly all the Bunk 6 girls felt uncomfortable. Silence prevailed for the remainder of the meal. They didn't know what to say. At last, the girls finished their breakfasts and trudged back to their cabin. They quietly sat on the lower bunk beds.

"Girls, remember, we have a cabin to clean," reminded Susan as she pointed to clothes and towels scattered on the floor, comic books strewn about, and unmade beds. "You don't want your parents to see you living like this. Do you?"

"Sure, why not?" snickered Micky. "We do it at home. We don't want them to think we've changed too much. How much longer do we have to wait before our parents arrive?"

Susan responded, "It's 8:15 so you have less than two hours. Come on, let's clean up. Mitzi said every cabin had to be perfect before you could join your parents."

With the last announcement, the girls jumped to their feet. Micky strode over to the job chart hung on the end of the shelves. Susan assigned each girl a different chore daily. Micky read their tasks from the list.

"Lynn, you have first sweep. Ann, you are second sweep. Donna, you have the porch. Janie, you have the bathroom. I am the cubby hole inspector and bed checker," Micky announced.

"I had bathroom two days ago," whined Janie. "It isn't fair."

"No, you couldn't have," interrupted Donna. "You don't have the same job for five days."

"Quit arguing, you two," demanded Lynn. "Why don't you just go to work?"

"Why don't you mind your own business," retaliated Donna.

"Now, girls," Susan interrupted, "This won't help at all. I know you're angry because you're tense and anxious to see your parents. However, that doesn't get your jobs completed. I want all of you to start to work. Right now."

The girls started their jobs, working slowly and carelessly. Susan noticed they seemed indifferent. Lynn pushed the dust and dirt from one corner of the room to the other, without first picking up clothes lying on the floor. Donna, while waiting for the broom to sweep the porch, sat on her bed reading a comic book. Janie splashed water around in the bathroom.

"All right, everyone, stop," shouted Susan. "Lynn, it seems to me, by now you should know clothes are to be picked up before you sweep."

"All she is doing is getting our clothes dirty," accused Janie.

"If you kept your clothes off the floor, you wouldn't have to worry," answered Lynn sarcastically.

"Why don't you pick them up?" hissed Micky.

"Because I'm busy," spat Lynn. "Why don't you? You have the easiest job of all."

Ann blurted out, "Why do we have to have a silly inspection today, anyhow?"

"Girls, enough. Stop this bickering now. Ann, help Lynn pick up the clothes. Donna, give me the comic book." The child looked at her and went on reading. "I said give it to me." Susan was really angry, This was one of the few times that summer that she had been irate at all the campers' behavior.

She stormed over to Donna and grabbed the comic book, demanding, "Get the mop and mop the porch. Micky, help the others. I want your beds and cubby holes neat. Janie, quit making a bigger mess in the bathroom and clean it properly. If I hear any more quarreling among you, everyone will be docked from her favorite activity."

They now realized their counselor meant what she said, and all of them actively cooperated in finishing their jobs. Anxious to be with their parents, Bunk 6 knew the cabin must be immaculate before they could join them. Nerves snapped and tensions built. In about a half hour, they finished.

Inspection took place from 9:15 until 9:45. Mitzi stopped at each cabin to examine the buildings thoroughly. She criticized whenever she found an unsatisfactory job. After she checked all the cabins, Mitzi returned to those needing extra work. She made sure all problems had been corrected before she allowed campers to go to the rec hall. It was there that everyone congregated before Visitors Day started.

The girls waited impatiently, grumbling that it was unfair for Visitors Day hours not to start earlier.

Susan spoke gently, "It only seems you have been waiting a long time. I can remember how time dragged when I was a camper."

Micky interrupted her. "Susan, we know all about when you were a camper. Do we have to be reminded again? Give us a break," she fumed.

"Of course not," responded Susan. "I'm sure Mitzi will be here soon. It's 9:30."

A few minutes later, Mitzi called through the door, "I wanted to save my better cabins for the last inspections. Are you all ready?"

The girls nodded and stood by their beds.

"I know how anxious you are to see your parents," she continued, "I hope you will introduce them to me."

Some nodded again while others sighed.

Mitzi went through the cabin inspecting each cubby hole and bed. "Did you pull out all your clothes and thoroughly clean the cubby holes or did you only straighten them?"

"They did the messy ones all over again. Most were very neat," Susan explained to Mitzi.

"Well, they look fine. Your beds, bathroom, porch, floors, everything looks good. Let me check one more thing though." She ran a finger over the top of the cubby hole shelves in search of dust.

"No dirt there," she announced. "Girls, you did a good job on your cabin. I can't find anything to criticize so I won't need to come back again. Everyone is gathering at the rec hall. Susan, please take your campers there now."

"All right, Mitzi. Come on, girls, let's go."

Bunk 6 could barely keep from running to the building. In a few minutes, the clock hands would point to 10:00 a.m. Soon the waiting would end, and they would be with their loved ones. Everyone impatiently watched the large clock on the rec hall's back wall. Just before the time to go to the gate, Mrs. Warren stood on the rec hall stage, calling for everyone's attention.

"Girls and boys, I am pleased to see all of you dressed in your camp uniforms. Your directors have given me excellent reports about your inspection today. I'm delighted. Please keep your cabins clean for the rest of the day. Since I'd like to say 'Hello' to as many parents as possible, please bring them over to me." She glanced at her watch. "I see it's time to go to the gate. You are free to join your families. Have a wonderful time."

The campers emitted shouts of joy and raced toward the gate to greet their parents. Susan's girls stayed together hoping their parents had already arrived. Susan remained at the rec hall where she had been assigned the duty of helping to serve cold drinks and distribute name tags to arriving families.

Her girls became disappointed when they realized their parents weren't among the first to arrive. Constant shouting occurred when other campers recognized their parents followed by hugs and kisses and questions.

"I wish my parents were here right now," whined Donna.

"I do, too. My parents should know Visitors Day starts at ten o'clock. It doesn't seem right for other parents to be here on time and ours to be late," complained Micky.

The others agreed, except Lynn. She announced, "Since my parents aren't coming, I think I'll join Susan at the rec hall and then go back to the cabin to read."

Ann gave her a sympathetic look. "I'll see you later, Lynn."

Lynn nodded and plodded up the dirt path to the rec hall. She felt unhappy and left out of the excitement around her. She wished her parents had saved their visit for today rather than coming earlier. It just wasn't fair. Why was Europe so important to them, anyway? She walked over to Susan and asked if she could help her.

"Not right now, Lynn. Have any of the parents from our group arrived?"

She shook her head. "I'm going back to the cabin to read."

Susan immediately sized up the situation and answered, "All right, Lynn. We'll do something together when I'm finished here. Come on, cheer up."

Lynn wandered out of the building, with her head down, peering mournfully at the ground. At the cabin, she lay on her bed, crying as if all the world had come to an end. "It just isn't fair," she sobbed. "I want my parents to be here, so much."

Meanwhile, many other parents had arrived but not the families of Bunk 6. At last, Micky recognized a car coming down the camp road. She ran to the gate and waited.

"Hey, gang," she blurted out, "I think my parents are here."

She was correct. The Reiners, Micky's parents, parked their car and came toward the gate. They waved to Micky. At last, she was in their arms.

"Gee, it's good to see you, Mom and Dad. Did Ellen come?" Ellen was Micky's five year-old sister who Micky had helped raise since the child was born.

"No, honey. They only allowed children over twelve years of age to come on Visitors Day this year. We left Ellen with one of her friends," her mother informed her.

Disappointed for a moment, Micky then perked up. "I can't wait to take you to the stables. They have the cutest horse this year. I rode him last year, too. His name is Sprinter. Or, would you rather walk around the entire camp?"

"No, dear, we saw it last year. I'd like to see what you made in arts and crafts, though," suggested her father.

"Fine, Dad. First, let's go see Sprinter. O.K.?"

"Absolutely," her father smiled, and the three headed for the stables hand-in-hand.

A short time later, Donna's parents, the Winters, arrived. She rushed toward them, almost knocking over her mother, and scrambled into her father's arms.

"Donna, you look terrific," commented her father as he hugged her.

"You must have grown two inches," her mother smiled happily, "and you're thinner. Camp must be agreeing with you. It is wonderful to see you again, dear."

The child cried happy tears. She was very close to her parents and overjoyed at seeing them.

"What are you crying for, angel?" observed her father. "Come on, I'm anxious to meet your counselor. You have written so much about her."

They strode over to the rec hall. Donna pointed to Susan, and her parents walked over to her.

"Hello, Mr. and Mrs. Winters, I'm Susan Grant. I've heard so much about you."

"Thank you, Susan. Donna writes constantly about you and about how much she enjoys camp. Mr. Winters and I have been eager to meet you."

"Thank you very much. It's been wonderful having your daughter in my group. She's a fine camper." She handed them their name tags and the summer's first edition of Camp Floridian's newspaper. "Camp Floridian is giving out name tags to every parent so families can get to know each other."

"Thank you," smiled Mr. Winters. "Do you go to college, Susan?"

"I'm a sophomore at the University of Miami." She addressed the child, "Donna, why don't you show your parents around camp. I think they would like that."

"All right, Donna, give us the Cook's Tour." Mrs. Winters inquired, "Will we see you later, Susan?"

"You will. Have a good time." Susan waved goodbye.

Janie strolled over to Susan with her family. "Hello, Mr. and Mrs. Barnes," greeted Susan. "You must be Janie's brother, Donald. I'm happy to meet you."

"Yeah, but my name is Don not Donald." He was a handsome boy of about seventeen. "Hey, you're not bad looking. Are you doing anything later?"

"Sorry. I'm busy," Susan slowly replied. The boy did not seem to have any manners. "Did you know Janie was in the camp talent show and play, Mr. and Mrs. Barnes? She was wonderful."

"My Don was the star of the play when he went to camp," huffed Mrs. Barnes. "I expected the same of Janie. I didn't expect her to be just an assistant."

"Yes, that certainly was a disappointment," agreed Mr. Barnes.

"Hey, Susan," inquired Don. "did the kid do well in the talent show? I was the top act in mine when I attended camp."

Susan took a deep breath. "Oh, really!" She tried hard to control her anger. "Your sister was marvelous in both shows. I was very proud of her. We'd like all parents to wear name tags, and here is one for Don. Janie, why don't you give your parents a guided tour around camp? It was nice meeting you, Mr. and Mrs. Barnes."

As she returned to her job of pouring drinks, she reflected, "Janie sure has a conceited brother. Poor kid! Her parents act as if she is supposed to follow in his footsteps. No wonder Janie is so shy. She must feel inadequate."

The Reiners, after hiking to the stables, came to the rec hall. They, like all parents, were anxious to meet their daughter's counselor. Micky had told them her name, and they strolled over to her.

"You must be Susan," Mrs. Reiner introduced herself.

"Yes, I am. Your daughter is an exceptionally fine camper, Mr. and Mrs. Reiner. I'm so glad to have her in my cabin."

"Thank you. Micky has always liked camp. Haven't you, dear?" Mrs. Reiner noted.

Micky nodded. "Susan is the best counselor I've ever had."

"Why thank you, Micky." Susan was slightly embarrassed. "Has Micky shown you around the camp yet, Mr. and Mrs. Reiner?"

"Yes, we saw it last year. We liked it so much we decided Micky should come back this year. I saw the work she did in arts and crafts. It seems to me the campers are completing fantastic projects. I especially like the earrings Micky made," Mrs. Reiner observed.

"Yes, she does well in crafts. Micky is also leader of her cabin group." Susan gave them their name tags and excused herself as she returned to pouring punch. Although she would have liked to have spent additional time with each of her girl's parents, she had her assigned responsibility. Besides, Visitors Day was for campers not counselors.

Ann waited at the road near the gate. Her mother had not yet arrived. By now, most of the other parents had come.

"Why isn't my mother here yet?" she brooded. "It must be past 10:30."

Ann recognized her mother's car as Mrs. Davis drove it into the lot and parked. She waved to her daughter, who hurried to her side. She was a beautiful woman, very tall and thin, the type who looked like a model.

"Gee, Mom, I'm glad to see you. I expected you earlier. How come you're so late?" Ann greeted her.

"Darling, I thought parents weren't allowed into camp until after 10:30. I'm sorry." She turned her daughter around, her eyes expressing the love she felt for her.

"You look wonderful. Oh, I have good news for you. I sold one of my paintings and bought some statuary with the money. You'll love it. Let me see what you have been doing this summer. I remember you wrote me how much you love your arts and crafts classes."

"Sure, Mom. First, I want you to meet Susan. That's my counselor. You'll like her."

"I'm sure that I will. Which way do we go?"

"The rec hall is on this road." Ann led her mother toward the building.

When they arrived, Susan was still busy but soon took a break and hurried over to them. "Hello, Mrs. Davis, I'm sorry I was busy when you came in. I've been anxious to meet you."

"I'm so glad to meet you. Please call me 'Joan.' Ann has been writing to me regularly about camp. She especially likes arts and crafts."

"Ann is very talented. The arts and crafts counselor, Jean Meadows, and I are very surprised with her work. She talks constantly about painting."

"I'm glad she has done some top notch work this summer. I've tried to bring culture into our home by buying paintings and sculpture, by taking Ann to museums, and by giving her painting lessons. I'd like to see the arts and crafts building. Where is it located?"

"It's close by. First, though, I would like to give you a name tag. Ann, why don't you show your mother the rest of the camp? I think she might enjoy seeing it. I'll see you later, Joan."

The two wandered out of the rec hall. Susan continued to work until another counselor relieved her an hour later. Susan had now met all the parents of her campers. For the most part, except for Janie's family, they seemed like very nice people.

She returned to the cabin where she found Lynn reading a book. "Lynn," she broke in, "I'm through working. Do you want to go swimming?"

"No, thanks, Susan. I want to read. I don't want to pretend you're taking the place of my parents. Besides, I'll be busy later with the water show."

"Be sure to tell me if you want to do anything later." Susan walked over and tried to put her arm around her, but Lynn squirmed away.

"I know how it feels, Lynn. My parents couldn't come to the camp where I was when I was eleven. I was in North Carolina that summer. I was very unhappy about it and felt no one in the world cared about me. But I was wrong, Lynn. One of my bunkmate's parents took their daughter out for dinner and asked me to come with them. I forgot to concentrate on my parents, and I had a lot of fun. You see, I had forgotten why they hadn't come. It wasn't because they didn't want to; they just couldn't travel such a distance for one day."

Lynn fell into Susan's arms and cried. Afterwards, she wiped away her tears. "Susan, thanks for understanding. I think I'm ready to do something now."

Susan glanced at her watch and shook her head. "All we have time for is lunch. I'm sorry. I didn't realize it was so late. Come on, Lynn, let's get over to the mess hall."

Lynn looked sadly at the ground then at Susan. "That's all right," she sighed. "I'm not sure I wanted to do anything, anyways," she added. The two left the cabin and strolled over to the dining hall where many were waiting outside.

After the lunch whistle blew, visitors and campers started to slowly enter the mess hall where staff served box lunches of chicken and beverages. Lynn and Susan entered the line to wait for their food. After a long delay, they received their meals. They then hunted for two empty spaces at one of the tables. Parents and children sat together, talking among themselves or with others seated nearby.

Lynn and Susan found a place to sit and started eating. The chicken was delicious, a definite change from sandwiches served at most camps during Visitors Day.

Ann and her mother spotted Susan and came over to join her. "Susan, I'm pleased with the work Ann has done in arts and crafts. I'm surprised, though, that Camp Floridian doesn't offer more painting," commented Mrs. Davis, as she was having her lunch.

"Joan, the sketch class they offer during optional periods, when the children choose their activities, is supposed to take care of this need. They do have watercolors and oils for the older campers. I want you to meet one of Ann's bunkmates. This is Lynn Kingston."

"Hello, Lynn. Aren't your parents here yet?"

"Hello. They aren't coming. They're in Europe," moped Lynn, in between bites of food.

"Ann, why didn't you tell me you had a bunkmate whose parents weren't here? Lynn, how about spending the day with us? We'd love to have you join us."

"No, thank you," Lynn declined, staring at her plate. "I have plans for today. I'm in the water show."

"That's right. The instruction sheet I received did mention a water show. Are you in it, Ann? I'm anxious to see you swim."

"I'm in one of the races," Ann responded.

Since a continuous line of people entered the mess hall, it became impossible to speak without shouting. To make themselves heard, Lynn, Susan, and the Davis family went outside after lunch to sit on one of the aluminum bleachers set up for the day.

They talked at length. Mrs. Davis told them about Europe. She had traveled throughout the Continent for two summers on a painting binge and had enjoyed her trips. She had been impressed with Europe's beauty, particularly Greece. Mrs. Davis told them how pleased she was with the Visitors Day program at Camp Floridian. She ended by saying, "Lynn, I'll be watching you in the show. If you change your mind, please join us."

At 1:00 p.m., Mrs. Warren blew her whistle and announced, "All campers have to return to their cabins for a forty-five minute rest period." This was met with a chorus of groans and unwilling goodbyes.

"Parents can go anywhere around the campus during rest hour except the cabin areas. I'll be happy to answer any questions you may have about our camp," Mrs. Warren concluded.

All the campers, unhappily, left for their cabins. After Bunk 6 returned to theirs, the girls reported what their parents had seen.

"Remember, I said I was taking my parents to the nature cabin?" grinned Donna. "I picked up the jar holding the garter snake to show my parents. Well, when my mother saw the snake, boy, did she jump. She told me to put the jar down immediately because the snake might crawl out. Is she ever scared of them," she chuckled. "Susan, they thought you were very nice."

"My parents liked what I did in arts and crafts," commented Micky. "I didn't take them all around our camp as they saw it last year. Susan, mine thought you were special, too. They said they could see why I like you."

"Mom thought you were intelligent. She doesn't say that about many people," Ann enthusiastically pointed out. "She wants me to do more painting while I'm here. Otherwise, she thinks it is a good camp. I know I like it."

"What did your parents think of the camp, Janie? I saw you with them and your brother. Wow is he sharp looking," Micky added.

Janie stared angrily at her and spat out, "My brother may be good looking, but he is very conceited. He has the manners of an ox. All my parents ever do is compare me with him. If I'm not as good as he was in camp, they make a special point of rubbing it in. I hoped they would be happy to see me. The only one they care about is Don."

Janie added, "I guess they thought the camp was all right. They didn't say much about it or about you, Susan, although Don did. He said you were pretty but not his type. I wish I was in Lynn's place. I wish they would leave."

After comforting Janie, Susan said, "I enjoyed meeting all of your parents, girls. Did you introduce them to your bunkmates?"

"I didn't see anyone from our cabin," explained Donna.

Susan learned that no one else had except Lynn. Micky had only seen Janie from a distance.

"I'll have my parents meet everybody later," assured Micky.

While the campers rested in their cabins, parents had an opportunity to walk around the camp, meet each other, or ask questions of counselors who taught various activities. They became anxious to be with their children. However, camp had its rules and regulations. Neither campers nor parents could tamper with these rules. Rest hour seemed like forever. Time dragged as it had when the campers waited for Visitors Day.

The last ten minutes of the rest period, Susan called out, "Girls, since the water show will take place immediately after rest hour, I suggest you change into your bathing suits now." The girls quickly agreed and started to prepare for the show.

"Hey, everybody, I just remembered to tell you. My parents brought a huge box of candy," announced Micky, excitedly.

"My mother did, too," broke in Ann. "Tonight is party night."

The whistle ending rest hour finally blew, and campers hurried to join their parents to escort them to the lake. Benches had been set up for the visitors with plenty of space upon the ground for campers to sit.

Jerry stood on the docks. After everyone was seated, he called for their attention. "Good afternoon, I'm Jerry Martin, the camp's waterfront director. I want to welcome all you campers, visitors, and counselors to our annual water show. Today, we will have races. In addition to this, we will present two new events. Camp Floridian will offer, for the first time, a water ballet presented by our thirteen and fourteen-year-olds of Bunks 11 and 12. We will also have a special water-skiing exhibition by our own champion skiing instructor, Jack Kelley, and five of our best skiers.

"Our swimmers are classified as beginners, intermediates, swimmers, advanced, and junior lifesavers. Of course, the better the swimmer, the higher the ranking. Each grade teaches improvement of four basic strokes: crawl, sidestroke, breaststroke, and backstroke. We also instruct diving. Before we start the races, we will have various campers illustrate these strokes. Will the campers who will carry out this portion of the program please come forward. Thank you."

The campers skillfully demonstrated various swimming strokes. The participants received quite a few favorable comments from parents, as well as much hearty applause. Then the races began with all campers competing. The beginners came first; then the intermediates, until those in the advanced class took their turn. Although this part of the program took a lot of time, Mrs. Warren felt it was worthwhile since parents always seemed interested in seeing how well their children swam.

Next came the campers, including Lynn, who gave water-skiing exhibitions. The girls of Bunk 6 proudly told their parents that she was in their cabin.

Jack followed by performing various tricks and jumps on skis. He gave an exciting performance bringing ooh's and ah's from the crowd. It was no wonder campers learned to ski well when they had an instructor as talented as Jack Kelley.

At last, the show's portion began for which many parents had been waiting. They knew water ballet was a sport which when performed well was precise and beautiful to watch. The fourteen campers jumped, as one, off the dock into the lake. They swam with graceful synchronized strokes, dipping under the water then mightily breaking the surface with legs held high. They made a breathtaking picture. As they came out of the water, everyone gave them a standing ovation. Their performance showed the results of hard work and expert coaching.

As the campers returned to their cabins to change into dry clothes, they talked about the water pageant. It had been a terrific show. All the parents seemed pleased their children were learning the fundamentals of swimming.

They then introduced their parents to their bunkmates. Bunk 6's parents were delighted to meet Susan's other campers. Besides spending the day with their youngsters, it was always important for families to meet a child's counselor and cabin mates.

The remainder of the afternoon passed too quickly. Most visitors started to leave at 5:00 since, for many, it was a long drive back to their homes.

Ann's mother had wanted to stay, but she had a lot of painting to do since she had a gallery exhibit due in four weeks. Ann understood. Art was important in both their lives. Before she left, Mrs. Davis informed Ann that she had talked to Jean about increased opportunities for Ann to draw and paint. Jean had assured her something would be worked out.

Janie was glad to see her parents leave. They had criticized her for coming in fourth in the race instead of first or second. They, again, compared her to Don, making the situation even worse.

A few parents agreed to have dinner at camp. Donna coaxed hers to do so. The Reiners intended to spend the night in Orlando. This allowed them some extra time with their daughter.

Soon dinner was over. Mrs. Warren announced that the remaining visitors must leave. Micky quickly joined Susan and most of her bunkmates. She was an experienced camper and easily said goodbye to her parents. However, Donna pulled her parents off to an area where they could be alone. She started crying when they said that they were leaving.

"Donna, you'll be home in three weeks. You know how fast the last five weeks went," soothed her father, trying to console his child.

"I don't care. I don't mind camp. I only want to be with you."

"Listen, dear, we can't take you home. We've already paid for the eight weeks session. Be a big girl. You're ten years old. We want you to finish the camp season," insisted Mrs. Winters.

Donna continued to cry. She was once again homesick and wanted her parents.

"We'll write to you. Before you know it, you'll be home and wanting to go back to camp. Donna, we are about the only ones left, and we have to leave. Come on, how about a smile," coaxed Mrs. Winters.

As her parents kissed her and started toward their car, Donna emitted a forced smile and waved good-bye. Regretfully, she joined Susan and the other girls as they returned to their cabin to rest. It had been a big day. Perhaps, they might even have a bunk party later.

Chapter Fourteen

Lazy Day and Robin Hood

When Donna reached the cabin patio, she decided not to follow her bunkmates inside. Instead, she leaned against a cabin porch post, gazed toward the lake, and cried softly. Susan heard her camper weeping, got off of her bed, and walked outside. She was hoping to comfort her.

"What's wrong, Donna?" she called gently from the doorway.

Donna looked up for a moment then continued staring toward the lake.

She reached Donna's side and put an arm around her. "You did very well today coming in second in the race. I was very proud of you. You have really learned how to swim this summer."

The child stood there, her eyes fixed on the lake, rubbing her face with her hand. Tears continued to flow, tears of loneliness and unhappiness.

After a few minutes, Susan turned Donna around to face her. "Do you remember how much you wanted to go home when you first arrived at camp? You thought that without TV or parents that you wouldn't have much fun. I recall after you became busy with activities that you didn't have much time to think about television or movies or any other luxuries you have at home. You became too busy with the camp play and plans for the overnight. You learned to swim and went to nature classes. Haven't you had a good time this summer?"

Donna nodded and wiped away more tears. "I know those weeks went fast, but three more weeks seem like such a long time. I'll be all right, Susan," she sniffed.

She thought for a moment and added, "Besides, the big events happened during the last five weeks. There's nothing special that I can look forward to during the rest of camp."

"That's where you're wrong. We have the Robin Hood Tournament on Tuesday. Remember, Marla told you about it. After that, we have Color War for five days next week. Right before we go home, we have the prom and farewell banquet. Camp has more special events after Visitors Day than before it. You'll be very busy, and I'm sure you'll have a good time. In fact, that's a promise." She reached over and gave Donna a hug.

Donna stopped crying and hugged her counselor back. She seemed pleased that Susan was so understanding.

"Now, why don't you join our bunk party inside," encouraged Susan. "We have candy and pretzels. I think there may even be some potato chips left. It will be lots of fun. Only our bunk, no outsiders."

With Susan following behind, Donna brightened and strolled into the cabin. The other campers were tearing into food packages.

"Hey, Donna," offered Micky, "do you want any potato chips?"

"Of course," she admitted. "who doesn't?" Using a towel as a mat, she joined the others sitting in a large circle on the floor.

Micky's parents had brought two packages each of licorice and peppermint candies as well as a metal can of potato chips while Ann's mother had brought a large bag of pretzels and a two-pound box of chocolate candy. It was indeed a feast to relish. Three meals a day were fine for nutritious food. However, on Visitors Day, campers always appreciated packages of junk food. Each girl received equal amounts of all the snacks.

"Hey," announced Micky, "I got a terrific idea. I like potato chips better than candy, so why don't we trade what we don't like?"

"That's a good idea. I'll give five pretzels for two peppermints," bartered Ann.

"Nothing doing!" exclaimed Janie. "You'll have to give me eight pretzels if you want any peppermints from me."

"Tell you what, Ann. I'll give you a peppermint for four pretzels," piped up Lynn.

That seemed to be the best offer, and the two campers completed the trade.

"I'll swap ten potato chips for two pieces of chocolate," bid Donna.

"Fine," agreed Micky, greedily licking salt from the potato chips off her fingers. "My face is beginning to break out." She pointed to a single pimple on her forehead.

The food was delicious and the perfect touch for the end of an enjoyable day. Besides, they couldn't afford to have food found by Mitzi since packages of goodies were prohibited in cabins. If campers received food, it had to be eaten immediately or hidden from the prying eyes of directors. This problem was best solved by an instantaneous bunk party.

They discussed Visitors Day and the water show. Micky had won the race for beginning swimmers. She had jumped off the dock quicker than the others and left them far behind as she reached the dock on the other side of the swimming area.

Lynn had easily skied all the way around the lake. Before camp, she had taken several private lessons; now with Jack's help, Lynn was becoming quite accomplished. During camp's remaining time, she hoped to learn to ski with one ski. That would be difficult to master. However, Lynn seemed to learn any water sport quickly.

Perhaps, because their parents had brought news of them, Bunk 6 also discussed their friends back home. Micky reported her little sister, Ellen, would enter the first grade in the fall and was actually looking forward to school.

"Poor kid," sympathized Lynn, "she doesn't know how miserable school is."

This brought on a debate about whether school was fun or not. Ann liked it, especially when she had art classes. Micky endured school. The rest of the campers did not like education at all. Donna complained that schoolwork was too difficult.

When she heard this, Susan couldn't help but laugh. She had felt the same way Donna did when she was in elementary school. Now, however, Susan enjoyed taking courses. Senior high had been fun, and college was exciting. It was wonderful to choose subjects in which she was interested, and she had developed into an excellent student. Perhaps, this was because she found university classes stimulating.

The girls continued to eat while talking. They discussed entering fifth grade in the fall and in two years being ready for junior high. Janie inquired, "Susan, what was seventh grade like? Do you remember?"

"I don't look that old, do I, Janie?" Susan chuckled. "Let's see, in junior high, you don't have the same teacher all day long nor do you have as many subjects to learn. It's more difficult than elementary school."

"Hey, you do remember," teased Janie. "I thought someone your age would forget. I mean you're in college."

"Oh, some things haven't slipped my mind." Susan looked at her watch and realized it was 8:30. "Such as it's time for you to get ready for bed. Lights go out in half an hour."

The girls looked puzzled. Had time gone by so quickly? It didn't seem possible.

"It's 8:30," Susan explained. "I suggest you clean up the floor. Get rid of all the bags and candy wrappers. I'd like a volunteer to sweep the cabin."

No one moved as they preferred to have a thorough cleanup the following morning. "We have flies in this cabin every so often, and I don't want a family of ants moving in," pointed out Susan. "Micky, you had the easiest job this morning. I want you to sweep." The child nodded and went to get the broom.

"The rest of you get undressed," Susan ordered.

The campers traipsed quietly over to their cubby holes to get their night clothes. Although the party had alleviated some of the letdown of their parents leaving, the girls suddenly felt a little lonely and homesick.

When the cabin had been swept and her campers prepared for bed, Susan announced, "Girls, I have a surprise for you. Tomorrow is Lazy Day. You don't have to get dressed or go to the mess hall for breakfast. Cereal and milk will be delivered to our cabin. In fact, you can stay in your pajamas until 11:00 when everyone goes for general swim."

Smiles lit up the girls' faces. They grew more relaxed and happier. Tomorrow would be fun. It would be great to loll around in bed all morning. Her campers soon fell asleep with Susan joining them in slumber. It had been an exhausting day, full of action. She was too tired to go to the lodge.

No one blew Reveille the next morning. However, perhaps because of habit, some Bunk 6 girls awakened at the usual time. When they realized it was Lazy Day, they quickly closed their eyes and fell back to sleep. Quiet breathing filled the cabin room. It wasn't until 10:00 a.m. that all awoke.

Susan stood on the patio, eagerly anticipating the old, blue pickup truck delivering their breakfast. She didn't have to wait long as the truck rolled along the side of Bunk 6 and came to a gentle stop. It was a welcome sight for campers and counselor since they had all started to experience a few hunger pangs.

Ben, the camp's truck driver, mumbled, "How many individual cereal boxes do you want and how much milk?"

"We need six packages of cereal and two quarts of milk," responded Susan.

"Lynn, Janie, I need some help," she shouted. The girls exited the cabin, and the three of them ambled over to get the supplies from Ben.

"Thanks, Ben," she called back, as they quickly carried the food into the cabin.

The girls once again formed a circle on the floor as they had last night at the party. They poured cereal into bowls, added milk, and munched away happily. It was like being on a picnic.

After she finished eating, Janie inquired, "Susan, I'm still sleepy. Can I go back to bed?"

"Sure, if you want to," agreed Susan, "but only for about fifteen minutes. We still have cleanup today." There was a chorus of groans.

"The good news is," Susan continued, "we don't have an inspection." The groans instantly turned to cheers.

"You know what, Susan?" grinned Lynn. "They should hold Lazy Day every week." The child yawned, followed by laughter and complete approval from the other campers.

"I don't know, Lynn. I have a feeling you wouldn't like it," cautioned Susan. "I'll bet you would probably get tired of having Lazy Days if you had more than one."

"No, we wouldn't," disagreed Donna. "How can you get tired of doing nothing? It's like having a holiday."

"Girls, don't you think you would get tired of Thanksgiving if you had one each month?" inquired Susan of her charges.

"Not me," giggled Janie. "I love turkey."

Susan decided to stop commenting and lay on her bed. Shortly afterwards, the girls grudgingly cleaned the cabin before leaving for general swim.

Since she had not seen Jerry in four days, Susan couldn't wait to go to the waterfront. They had both been extremely busy, particularly Jerry, as he had the responsibility of preparing and presenting the water show.

"Hi," he greeted her as they arrived at the lake. "Don't forget. We can take our day off after lunch is over. Where would you like to go?"

Susan thought for a moment. "I almost forgot today was Monday," she answered. "I think I would like to stay around camp. I'd love to place my girls under the care of a staff assistant and lie on our beach the rest of the afternoon. I'm still recovering from yesterday."

"That sounds like a great idea. Can I join you? Yesterday was a big day for me, too. Maybe we can go out for dinner in Leesburg this evening."

"You're on. The show was fantastic. That's no surprise though. I knew it would be."

"I'm glad you were confident. I wasn't so sure. You know how dress rehearsals never go as well as the real thing."

They talked for a while longer. After general swim and lunch, Susan turned her girls over to Terry, one of the staff assistants, and headed back to the lake. Sometimes counselors did not leave camp on their day off. Instead, they spent their free hours at camp enjoying their favorite activities.

The two counselors spent the rest of the day relaxing. They took a motorboat out for about an hour before having dinner at one of Leesburg's family restaurants. Susan returned to her campers, feeling refreshed. She looked forward to tomorrow afternoon's Robin Hood Tournament.

Throughout the camp season, all the girls from ages eight through fourteen had learned some of the archery fundamentals during classes held twice a week. Many campers could hit the target with regular consistency. Tuesday afternoon, the best archers of the junior and senior divisions would be determined. Prizes would be distributed at the banquet, including trophies for the winners and ribbons for second and third place.

The boys' side of camp had been taking classes in riflery. They would hold contests on the rifle range at the same time and receive the same prizes.

Anticipating the tournament, Susan's girls eagerly awoke Tuesday morning. Since Marla had eased up on the girls, they began to be more enthusiastic about archery. Janie, in particular, became quite skilled. She was anxious to go to the archery range and compete. Nature and arts and crafts seemed to drag for her today. After lunch, it was time for the competition to begin.

After all the girls had arrived at the range, Marla announced, "Well, girls, now is the time for all of you to show what you have learned in archery this summer. You will each be given five arrows to shoot at your targets. You eight and nine-year-olds will shoot at targets twenty feet away. The rest of you will aim from thirty feet away. The highest score you can have is forty-five. Remember, each bull's-eye counts as nine points. Good luck and good shooting."

Bunkmates competed against each other as cabin after cabin shot their arrows. At last, it was Bunk 6's turn. Susan called them over and enthusiastically said, "Good luck, everybody. Now let's show the other campers what you can do."

Susan's campers carefully shot their arrows at the same time followed by a tallying of scores. To no one's surprise, Janie was the winner from her cabin with a score of twenty-five including one bull's-eye. The others in Bunk 6 did not fare as well since they received scores ranging from five to eighteen.

After they completed the round for their cabin, all her bunkmates gathered around Janie. "Nice shooting, Janie," called out Micky. "Come on. Win it for Bunk 6."

Ann added, "Hey, Janie, you were great. I had a feeling you would be the winner from our cabin. Good luck in competing against the other cabins."

"Thanks, Ann," Janie muttered. "I'll do my best. I hope I win the trophy. Maybe if I do, my parents will shut up about Don. He has never won an archery trophy."

"You'll do fine," Susan assured her. "Remember, keep your arm straight and don't get nervous. Concentrate on what you're doing, and I'll bet you'll win the junior division competition."

She became concerned, however, that Janie was more interested in winning a trophy because of her parents' reaction than personal satisfaction in a job well done. She would speak to her camper about it later.

Marla called all the cabin winners together from the junior and senior divisions after the initial competition had been completed. It was now 4:00 in the afternoon. In about one hour, all the winners of the tournament would be known.

"All right, girls," she announced. "You are now to shoot your five arrows as I call your name and cabin number. You've all done well to get this far in the contest, win or lose. Now let's see who the best archers are at Camp Floridian this summer." She called the junior camper winners, one at a time, starting with the one from the eight-year old cabin.

At last, it was Janie's turn. She aimed the first arrow as she heard cheers from her bunkmates. However, she became nervous. When she let the arrow go, it soared over the target's top. She took a deep breath and regained her composure, finishing the round with a score of thirty points, a better tally than her first five shots.

After she finished shooting, Janie hurried back to rejoin her bunkmates, feeling a little disappointed she had not scored higher. Now all she could do was wait as she sat on the grass to watch. Susan glanced over at her and said, "Congratulations, Janie. We're very proud of you."

"Thanks," Janie mumbled, shrugging her shoulders and chewing on a blade of grass. She waited impatiently for the next half hour as the arrows went flying through the air, usually landing in the large white target.

At last, the junior division contest was over. Janie strained to hear as Marla called for everyone's attention. Had she won? Had she represented her cabin well? Was the trophy hers?

"Girls, you have shown good marksmanship today. Since everyone has taken a turn, we can finally announce winners for the junior division. The third place winner for the junior division is Kim Tyler, nine years old, Bunk 5. The second place winner is Janie Barnes, ten years old, Bunk 6 and our winner is..." She paused. "Our winner is Debby Allison from Bunk 8, eleven years old, with a score of 35 points. Debby, you will receive your trophy at the banquet. Congratulations, girls, you've made lots of progress in archery this year."

Janie was miserable. She thought to herself, "I can't do anything right. Second place isn't good enough." She rose to leave, not interested in the final competition of the senior division. Then she heard Marla call her name and turned around as the counselor hurried to her side.

"Janie, you did very well considering you are only ten years old, and this is your first year at Camp Floridian. I didn't expect you to come in second since you didn't know anything about archery five weeks ago. You surprised me. Good luck next year." Marla turned back so she could finish the tournament.

Janie didn't answer and started to trudge through the field on her way to her cabin. She saw Susan and her bunkmates leaving and waited for them to catch up with her.

Susan was the first to speak. "Congratulations, Janie. You shot better than everyone in the cabin and also most of the other girls. That's excellent." She noticed the child was sullen. "Are you upset because you didn't win?" she continued.

Janie didn't reply but just kept walking, eyes straight ahead, hands in pockets.

As soon as they reached the cabin porch, Susan told the others to go inside as she wanted to talk to Janie privately. Alone on the patio, Susan approached her camper, who still sulked.

"Listen to me carefully, Janie," she started. "The most important thing about competing is doing your best. I know you tried hard. That's as important to me as you winning a trophy. I'm not saying it's easy to lose. I know that it isn't. But to kick yourself, just because you aren't a champion, is wrong. If you have put forth your best effort possible, opinions of parents, friends and even your bunkmates shouldn't matter.

"You also need to remember that good sportsmanship is very important when you play a game. I was disappointed that you didn't congratulate Debby. You didn't have to tell her she deserved to win because you were also great. However, you should have gone to her after Marla announced the winners and simply said, 'Congratulations, Debby.' It's too late to say anything to her now, but I want you to remember to be a good sport in the future.

"Now let's go inside the cabin. Your bunkmates want to tell you what a wonderful job you did. When you shot, they provided the loudest cheering section in camp this summer. We're all very proud of you."

The two walked over to the screen door and went inside. "Perhaps Janie has learned a valuable lesson," thought Susan. She hoped she had made Janie understand that good sportsmanship and making an effort were essential to good character. Counseling campers was sometimes difficult, yet rewarding, if they learned from their experiences.

Chapter Fifteen

Ann's Escapade

Since Visitors Day, Ann had talked endlessly about painting. She wanted to spend her days sketching and informed Jean of this. In order to channel Ann's interest, the arts and crafts counselor cooperated. Jean gave her paper on which to draw, before or after dinner, when she had no scheduled activities. Unfortunately, however, Jean's action had a negative effect. Instead of aiding in directing Ann's time, the paper only fueled the child's passion for art.

Susan was becoming concerned that Ann had changed from trying and enjoying all activities to talking only about art and only wanting to sketch and paint. She had discussed this with Jerry yesterday on their day off. He assured her there was no reason for worry. Ann was probably going through a stage.

They had traveled to Orlando where Jerry rented a motorboat at a marina and purchased bait at a bait and tackle shop. He had brought his own fishing rods and tackle. Even though they hadn't caught any fish, it had been a day of fun. As usual, they had discussed their campers and the other counselors.

During their conversation, Jerry had casually mentioned that Marla would no longer be interfering with their lives. The archery counselor now dated Frank Anders, the new riding counselor who had replaced Red.

They had also discussed Lynn. Susan had noted that Lynn had definitely changed into a pleasant youngster from the domineering and sarcastic child she had been at camp's start. She had come to respect Susan and wanted to be like her. Lynn realized the only way to be accepted was by showing friendship toward others. She had become much more sociable.

The other girls in Bunk 6, except Micky, now completely accepted Lynn. They included her in their activities and conversations. Lynn was also gradually gaining Micky's trust. However, Micky still felt Lynn needed to do something spectacular if they were ever to become close friends. What it would be, she didn't know.

A typical Tuesday morning led to what appeared to be a very quiet afternoon. Following their horseback riding class, they returned to their cabin to change clothes. Susan coaxed, "Hurry, girls. It's almost time for your optional activities."

"Susan, do we have to go? I'm tired, and it's so hot today," grumbled Micky.

"Of course, you have to go. I thought you liked ceramics, Micky. Come on, girls," encouraged Susan. She gently pushed them out of the cabin.

Ann, however, decided to sneak off rather than go to her activities. She took paper and pencils with her. Instead of participating in the optional periods which she had chosen, she headed for the woods. To Ann, it was so important to her to spend more time sketching than the hours allotted her for the remainder of camp. Besides, hadn't her mother told her to spend more time drawing?

Susan knew the schedule of all of her girls' activities. She didn't suspect anything when Ann left the cabin wearing a bathing suit and carrying a towel. She didn't notice that, under the towel, Ann had hidden her sketching equipment.

At four in the afternoon, when Ann had not returned to the cabin, Susan began to worry. It was unlike the child to be late. Ann had always been prompt before this. Had something happened to her? Susan waited for another fifteen minutes. As each moment passed, her fears grew. All the other campers had returned from their activities. Susan told the rest to stay in Bunk 6 and ran to the waterfront.

Susan noticed Jerry on the docks and called out to him, "Jerry, have you seen Ann?"

He walked over to her immediately. "I haven't. I thought it was unusual when she didn't appear for swimming because she has never missed a class. But, I didn't give it a second thought. Did she head in this direction when she left the cabin?"

"I didn't notice if she walked toward the lake. She wore a bathing suit, and I thought she headed here. I'm worried."

"No need to panic, yet. She hasn't been near the waterfront area or I would have seen her. Now calm down. I think it would be a good idea if you sent your campers in different places to search for her."

"Remember, I told you yesterday that all she has cared about is art. Even if she went sketching, instead of to her classes, she should be back by now. I didn't sense anything wrong. I can't believe I let this happen," Susan rambled on, ignoring Jerry's suggestion.

"Susan, will you please take it easy. Maybe she's already back at the cabin. Check to see if she has returned. If she hasn't, send your kids hunting for her and let me know. We'll take it from there."

Susan raced back to the cabin, frightened and upset. She asked herself, over and over, "Why would Ann do something like this?"

When she reached the cabin, Ann was nowhere in sight. "Has Ann returned yet?" she asked Micky.

"No," Micky replied. "Where do you think she is?"

"I don't know. I want each of you to search a different area of camp. Micky, go to the rec hall, mess hall, arts and crafts, and the nature cabin. Donna, check the stables. Janie, you go to the other girls' cabins and find out if she is there or if anyone has seen her. Lynn, I don't know where else she might be. Wait! Check the area near our camp boundary on the east side of camp. You know, the area around the lodge near the lake. There's nothing there but marshy grass. However, that's a good place to think or sketch. Now hurry. Get back here as soon as possible."

The four girls ran out of the cabin toward the designated places where they had been sent to search, and Susan dashed back to the lake.

"Jerry," Susan shouted when she reached the waterfront.

He came out of the shack where he was putting away equipment. "Was she at the cabin?" he asked.

Susan shook her head quickly. She was frustrated and fearful.

"Let's report this to Mrs. Warren," he insisted.

The two walked quickly over to the camp owner's office and told her their story.

"Jerry, why didn't you tell me one of the campers was missing during optional periods? You should have sent someone to notify me," she reprimanded him.

"All the counselors were busy with their classes. I didn't realize anything was wrong until Susan told me Ann was missing, Mrs. Warren."

"Well, I'm glad you came to see me. Susan, if your campers haven't found her, I'll send out a search party. You should know where your campers are from now on. Enough criticism for now. Right now, finding Ann is the important thing. I would advise you to wait at the cabin until right before dinner. Come see me at the mess hall if Ann isn't back by then."

While Jerry stayed at the office to continue talking to Mrs. Warren, Susan hurried back to her cabin. She worried more by the moment. What if Ann was hurt? She could not sit and wait but paced the cabin floor, her heart beating faster, her mind full of anxiety.

One by one, her campers returned. They couldn't find Ann anywhere. None of the campers, at any other cabin, could remember seeing her that afternoon. Perhaps, Lynn had found her. Lynn had not returned yet.

It was almost 5:00. The campers of Bunk 6 became quiet and very serious. They sat on the lower bunks looking at their counselor, then at the floor, trying to figure out any possible places where Ann might be.

"Why isn't Lynn back?" Susan asked herself. "Has something happened to her, too?"

"Do you think Ann has run away?" inquired Donna of no one in particular.

"No, she likes camp," Susan reminded them.

Susan reflected, "At least, I thought she was happy here. I can't think of any reason why she would suddenly leave."

"Has she said anything to you girls about not liking camp or given any indication she was unhappy about anything?" she inquired.

The girls shook their heads.

"Ann has talked a lot about painting. I know that. However, Jean said she would take her sketching Thursday nights after dinner. That should have satisfied her," Susan fretted.

She added, "Ann always goes to her activities. This isn't like her at all."

The clock read 5:10. Dinner took place at 5:30. Ann knew that. She also knew what time activities ended in the afternoon. Susan's anxieties and tensions increased, thinking about possible accidents which might have befallen her camper. These thoughts started to give her a headache. She told herself she must gain control of her fears. She had four other campers in addition to Ann. They needed attention, too.

She considered for a moment, "It isn't fair for me to neglect these girls while I'm worrying about Ann." However, being upset, she continued along the same lines of thought.

"But they're safe. All are here except Lynn. I have reason to be upset about Ann."

As she was leaving to report to Mrs. Warren again, Susan heard footsteps outside the cabin. She raced toward the door where she saw Lynn with an arm around Ann, who limped badly. Susan immediately went into action.

"Thank goodness you're back!" she exclaimed, giving a sigh of relief.

Susan and Lynn helped Ann to the closest bed. She sent Micky to tell Mrs. Warren that Ann had been found.

"Where, where did you find her, Lynn?" sputtered Susan.

"I remembered that she had only talked about painting lately. Ann loves nature. When I didn't find her where you sent me, I searched the woods behind the cabins and found her there. Ann told me she was getting ready to leave the woods when she heard the whistle blow for the end of activities. Anyhow, when she attempted to get up, she fell and twisted her ankle. She can barely walk on it."

Susan sent Donna for Nurse Robbins and said a silent prayer of thanks.

"Susan, I like my new sketches. Do you want to see them?" pleaded Ann.

Susan nodded dumbly, and Ann unrolled the paper on which she had made her drawings. After looking at them quickly, the counselor regained her composure and said sharply to Ann, "I'm absolutely furious with you and very disappointed. You were to go to activities, not the woods. You had the other girls in your cabin, Jerry, Mrs. Warren, and me all worried about you. Ann, you can forget sketching and arts and crafts for a week. You're docked from your drawing classes. As for arts and crafts, you can attend and assist, but you can forget about making any projects for at least a week. I've had it with your artwork.

"I want your solemn promise you will never again go off by yourself without telling me where you are going. You will also go to all of your activities. Do I make myself understood? Now promise me."

Ann looked forlornly at her counselor. "I promise. Please, Susan, I have to do artwork. I just have to," she begged.

"You blew it, kid," Susan shouted. "And don't even think of repeating today's performance." She turned away from her camper.

Nurse Robins knocked on the door and entered the cabin. Ann winced as the nurse removed her shoe to examine her ankle. It was badly sprained.

Micky returned a few minutes later. She moved towards Lynn and said apologetically, "Lynn, I'm sorry for the way I've treated you this summer. That was quick thinking on locating Ann. Honest, I'm sorry."

"I deserved it," shrugged Lynn. "Before I found out how to make friends, I was a real brat."

"Want to be pals?" asked Micky.

"Sure. Why not?" agreed Lynn. Now she was accepted by the entire group. Her father had been right. It was good to make friends. She wished, however, she had realized this at the beginning of camp. Well, maybe they could all come back to Camp Floridian next year and be in the same cabin again.

"Susan," informed the nurse, "I want to keep Ann in the infirmary tonight in order to treat her ankle. We need to get the swelling down. I'll have Jerry bring her to my place."

"Sure, Alice. Thank you."

Shortly afterwards, Jerry entered the cabin to carry Ann to the infirmary. He saw everything was under control again and smiled at Susan. A few days in sick bay and Ann would be fine. Susan was thankful this horrible episode was over. Perhaps, normalcy would return to her cabin.

At least some good had come from this experience. She noticed Lynn and Micky walking together toward the mess hall for dinner.

She could breathe more easily and relax. Taking care of five campers, instead of worrying about one, was comparatively effortless.

Chapter Sixteen

Junior Prom

During the seventh week, campers and counselors started to anticipate the banquet and prom with which the season always ended. Everyone felt a feeling of excitement since Camp Floridian closed in less than two weeks.

Swimming instructors worked enthusiastically to correct campers' strokes so campers could pass tests placing them in a higher swimming rank. During arts and crafts, campers chose final projects. In nature, classes consisted of lectures about stars, plants, and animals. In athletics, they played the usual sports.

The children also continued to attend their optional activities. There, too, counselors started completing various programs by perfecting the campers' skills. During Susan's classes, campers produced the final edition of Camp Floridian's newspaper.

Friendships continued to be formed. Since Ann's adventure on Tuesday afternoon, Micky and Lynn had become inseparable. Since Ann's release from the infirmary on Saturday, they sat together at meals and walked to activities together. They revealed to each other their fantasies and aspirations, including their hopes the boys would invite each of them to the prom. Susan was delighted that, at last, Lynn had become well adjusted to camp and living with other children.

During Saturday's rest hour, Mitzi came to the cabin to talk to Susan. She wanted to speak privately so the two went outside on the patio.

"Susan, I've noticed how well you handle children. You also have good ideas about camp programs. Mrs. Warren and I would like you to be in charge of the girls for the junior prom. The dance is scheduled for next Wednesday night from 7:00 until 9:00 p.m. You will have a male counselor to help you supervise. Mike has already signed up for the job. In addition, you will have a committee consisting of staff assistants and three counselors to assist with refreshments and decorations. Will you help us?"

Susan hesitated for a moment and answered, "I think I can do it, but wouldn't Jean be better suited for handling the job?"

"Jean is in charge of making the decorations. She'll also help you to plan a theme for the dance. We know you're qualified to manage this responsibility, which is why we considered asking you."

"In that case, I can't possibly refuse," smiled Susan. "Have you planned any meetings?"

"There will be one at the lodge tonight. If you have OD, please exchange with another counselor. I appreciate this, Susan."

Mitzi left and went to the other cabins to round up counselors for the two socials. There would be a senior prom for the campers from Bunks 7 through 14 while the junior prom would be held for Bunks 1 through 6. Each dance would have a separate group of counselors in charge of its planning. Jean was the exception. Since she was the camp arts and crafts instructor, she would supervise the decorations for both.

At 9:00 p.m., Susan left her girls and went over to the lodge. Fortunately she would not have OD for another night so she had free time to go to the meeting. She noticed five counselors and staff assistants, in addition to Mike, and recognized Jerry and Jean in the group.

"Welcome to the Junior Prom Counselor Service," Jerry jested when he saw her.

Susan chuckled and answered back, "Thanks, Mr. Welcoming Committee." She seated herself on a rocker and waited for the meeting to begin.

Mike became very businesslike. "I think everyone is here. Let's clarify what everyone is doing. Susan, you're in charge of the girls' division. Jean, you handle decorations. Jerry, you assist with the decorations; basically, we need your help in hanging them up, since I know you are busy with the waterfront. Pat, you're in charge of refreshments." Pat was the general counselor of Bunk 2. She was one of the counselors responsible for boating during optional periods. "I'm in charge of the boys' division. Does anyone have any ideas for the theme? Last year, we did Alice in Wonderland."

Everyone remained silent. Then Jean spoke up. "Why can't we have an early Halloween theme?" she suggested. "We can hang black and orange streamers and balloons from the ceiling and walls. Masks can serve as favors. Soft drinks, cake, and ice cream will be the refreshments. We carried out this theme at one of the camps where I was a counselor before Camp Floridian. The children enjoyed it."

Susan burst out excitedly, "What a wonderful idea."

Jean was an extremely creative person, whether it was art or ideas for parties. Susan wished she could be like Jean. Unfortunately, art was not her forte.

The other counselors offered several other ideas. One suggestion, a Hawaiian Holiday, was ruled better for the senior division. Grass skirts, leis, and large pasteboard palm trees were decorations, and green iced cupcakes and lemonade for refreshments represented this theme. The group decided Jean's idea was best for the Juniors, and they discussed preparations for an Early Halloween.

"Jean," announced Susan, "I just got an idea. In addition to having orange and black streamers, couldn't we make cardboard faces in various shapes and colors such as Halloween figures?"

"That's a good idea," answered Jean. The others thought about it for a few minutes and nodded in agreement.

"We have our theme and decorations planned. What about food?" reminded Jerry.

"I knew you would get to that," grinned Pat. "I think we should keep the idea of the theme. What about serving brown and orange frosted cupcakes, vanilla ice cream, all sorts of candy, and orange-ade? It would look like Halloween, I think."

Susan interrupted, "That would be great. I think the children would enjoy it. What kind of program shall we have?"

"How about having a dance?" suggested Mike.

"My boys are allergic to dancing," Jerry emphasized. "They would rather play with caterpillars. Besides, my general counselor and I will have enough trouble hauling them into the bathroom and getting them to take their showers. I think they ought to play games rather than dance."

"Jerry," chimed in Susan, "I think they won't mind dancing, especially when you tell them they'll have ice cream and cupcakes to eat."

The counselors and assistants laughed and Pat exclaimed, "Boys will be boys!"

"I think we should have both," spoke up Jean. "We can have games for those who don't want to dance and records for those who do. I agree with Susan. Some boys won't mind, and the girls will definitely want to dance."

The other five agreed as the meeting ended. They completed plans for what they hoped would be a successful prom for the younger campers. The counselors also decided to have another meeting the following Tuesday night. On Wednesday, they would decorate the rec hall.

Sunday was a wonderful day. Everything was peaceful at camp. Ann still limped around on her sprained ankle, but an ace bandage relieved the pressure enabling her to join others in their activities. She sat on the sidelines and cheered or acted as scorekeeper when they went to athletics and took an active part in other programs.

Monday night finally arrived. Susan did not have a day off because Mrs. Warren required for counselors to spend all of their available time with their charges during the last week of camp. However, after her campers had gone to bed, Susan wandered over to the lodge as she usually did when not on OD.

Mike noticed Susan when she entered the lodge and walked over to greet her. "Hi. I have some great news about the prom. Jean told me she has started making the decorations. I stopped by the arts and crafts building to see them before I came over here. They look terrific. She and the two staff assistants are doing a great job. I know the junior prom will be a huge success."

This news encouraged Susan. She had helped Pat with the refreshments menu and planned to help hang streamers from the ceiling and cardboard figures from the walls. Her main responsibilities, however, consisted of arranging the entertainment and seeing that the girls had an enjoyable evening.

She wondered if the boys would be as thrilled about having a social as her girls – probably not. Boys under the age of eleven, as Jerry had reminded her, would rather have pillow fights than dance any time. Susan was positive of one thing: ice cream and cupcakes would be hits with the campers.

The two talked about the prom, discussed how successful the two camp shows had been, and mentioned college. Mike, Susan learned, studied theater at the University of Miami and would be a senior this fall. Due to his goal of directing children's productions upon graduation, he had taken a job at a summer camp.

It was getting late. Susan said, "Good night" and wandered back to her cabin. Before she fell asleep, she reflected on the camp season. It had been fun to work with ten-year-olds. Of course, there had been some unexpected events which chilled her when she remembered them, such as Lynn's accident and the afternoon they thought Ann was lost. Overall, though, Susan had enjoyed this summer tremendously.

She now looked forward to the banquet and prom. When she recalled her experiences as a camper, these events and Visitors Day remained among her favorite memories. The campers and counselors always seemed to enjoy them. Unfortunately, however, despite the dance and banquet being fun, they also signified the ending of camp. She fell asleep regretting that the summer would soon be over.

After Tuesday's optional periods, Micky burst into the cabin and called to Susan, "Guess what, Susan? Gary has asked me to go to the prom with him. Oh, I'm so excited. It will be my first date." Micky happily hugged herself. Her other bunkmates, except for Lynn, looked at her as if she had suddenly gone mad. After all, what was so special about dating a boy?

"Micky, do you actually want to go out with a boy?" sputtered Janie, surprised at Micky's behavior.

"Why shouldn't I?" Micky responded. "You children wouldn't understand. Some boys are actually nice and can think about something more than playing football and collecting bugs. Gary is like that. Oh, I'm so happy."

Susan smiled and thought, "Kids grow up today faster than ever before. But a ten-year-old taking such an interest in the opposite sex?" She shook her head.

Excitement continued to grow in camp as the time for the proms and banquet grew near. The older campers eagerly looked forward to their dance. Squeals of joy emitted frequently from cabins when a girl announced she had been asked for a date.

Finally, it was Wednesday's rest hour. A staff assistant stayed with Susan's girls while she went to help decorate the rec hall. Bunk 6's counselor could hardly wait for the evening ahead and was eager to get started on preparing the building for the prom.

She met with some other counselors involved in planning the dance. They gathered streamers, ascended ladders, and started to hang decorations across the ceiling and around the walls in a festive manner. It seemed difficult to believe a pile of streamers, balloons, and cardboard figures could provide such a delightful atmosphere.

At the same time, camp cooks prepared the refreshments in the mess hall so Pat could bring them to the rec hall at 7:00 p.m.

The kitchen staff baked dozens of cupcakes. Everyone rushed to have their jobs finished on time.

The rest of the afternoon seemed to speed by. At dinner, after saying grace, the girls devoured spaghetti and meatballs.

"I can't wait until tonight," squealed Micky. "Ooh, it will be special to be with Gary."

"I can't wait to go either," announced Lynn. "I didn't get asked to go like you did, Micky. I hope someone asks me to dance."

"Aw, what's so special about a prom?" inquired Donna.

"Yeah," agreed Janie. "I'm not so sure I want to hang around with a bunch of dumb boys."

"Relax, girls," grinned Susan, trying to remember what it was like to be ten. "I'm sure you'll have a good time."

"Well, I won't," exploded Ann. "My ankle's still messed up. Alice said I can go, but I can't dance. What good is that? It's not fun at all sitting there. It's just not fair."

"I know. It's a bummer," sympathized Susan. "You'll still have fun dressing up and playing games."

The campers continued discussing the prom for the rest of dinner before scurrying back to the cabin to get ready.

At seven, Jerry and Mike, as well as two male staff assistants, arranged the rec hall tables in a square. Simultaneously, Pat, Susan, and two female staff assistants ran over to put out place settings, favors, and refreshments. Everything was completed.

Susan looked at the rec hall, smiled, and thought, "It's been challenging to turn this place into a fairyland of fun for one night. I think we've succeeded. There's plenty of room for dancing and games inside the square. If the campers cooperate, everything will turn out just fine." She rushed back to her cabin to make sure her girls had dressed.

Shortly afterwards, a few boy campers walked over to the girls' division to pick up their dates for the prom. They were handsome, dressed in suits and wearing ties. This was the cleanest they had been all summer. The girls wore party clothes. Their faces and hair were shining.

The boys seemed ill at ease when they called for their dates. They stood around self-consciously while waiting for girls to come out of their cabins. They shuffled from one foot to another or pulled at their ties. When their dates joined them, they quietly walked with them to the rec hall. The rest of the junior division campers came to the prom by themselves.

Jerry ambled over to Susan's cabin. He looked very handsome in white pants and a navy sports coat. "Susan, are you ready?" he called.

"One second, Jerry. I'll be right out." Almost immediately, dressed in a stunning emerald green cocktail dress, she opened the screen door.

"Wow," he greeted her, as he gave her a corsage. "You know, Susan, you're prettier tonight than I've ever seen you, if that's possible. Are you prepared for the prom? I told my boys about the refreshments when they balked at attending. That settled it. They'll do anything for ice cream and cake. Well, if you're ready, let's go."

Susan looked at him and let out a slow grin. Then they headed over to the rec hall.

The evening dragged. The boys seemed more interested in talking about sports than dancing. They had to be constantly prompted by Mike, Jerry, and the other male counselors to mingle with the girls. The girls waited impatiently at their tables for partners. Micky was the only camper in Bunk 6 who had more than two dances as she and Gary spent the entire evening together. Even games did not seem to break the ice because the boys did not wish to play.

To make matters worse, the seven and eight-year-old boys made paper airplanes out of napkins and flew them through the air--much to the girls' disgust and reprimands from counselors. Some of the older boys got into a fist fight which the counselors had to break up. In short, the evening was almost a disaster, and Jerry and Susan had no time for themselves.

The refreshments were the evening's only successful part. The campers greedily ate the ice cream and cupcakes and constantly asked for more. Fortunately, Pat was aware that children devoured refreshments and made certain seconds and thirds were on hand.

At last, to the counselors' relief, the clock's hands pointed to nine and the prom ended. Bunk 6's campers slowly rambled back to their cabin with no one except Micky saying a word.

"I had a great time," announced Micky. "Gary didn't mind dancing at all."

"Well, I didn't have a good time," complained Janie.

The others wholeheartedly agreed.

"I thought you danced at a prom. The boys were horrible. They absolutely refused to dance," Janie added.

"Yeah, they and their stupid airplanes," snarled Donna. "I'll bet they don't know napkins are used for wiping their hands. I saw one kid actually smear his dirty hands all over the wall."

The girls prepared for bed muttering about the prom. Susan was upset her girls had not enjoyed the evening.

She reflected, "Well maybe tomorrow's senior prom will be a success. After tonight, I'm not so sure they should have dances for younger campers. At least, the banquet, on Friday, should be more enjoyable for the girls." She turned out the lights.

Chapter Seventeen

The Banquet and Farewell

After breakfast and cleanup, Susan and the girls came to the waterfront for first period Thursday morning. Today was the big day for their final swimming tests. Micky hoped to pass hers and become an intermediate. Under Jerry's patient encouragement, she had totally overcome her fear of the water. The rest wanted to move to the swimmer's classification.

Jerry saw them as he came out of the small, white waterfront shack housing the kick boards, water-skis, and other water sports equipment. He carried a clipboard on which he had a typed sheet listing the necessary skills required to pass their tests.

"Hi," he greeted the girls. "Everyone ready?"

"I think so," said Donna. "Let's get to it."

"I am, too," agreed Micky. "When will we get our cards?"

"At the banquet," Jerry replied. "Since you are all prepared, let's see what you can do. Everybody get wet."

The girls waded enthusiastically into the water and looked at Jerry with great anticipation.

"All right, girls," he announced, as he approached the dock, "the first test I'm giving today is the intermediate. Micky, I want you to relax until I can give you your beginner's test. I'll be back to you shortly."

Micky nodded and Jerry continued, "The first stroke I want to see today is your crawl."

For the rest of the period, Susan and Jerry watched the campers go through their paces. Finally, they finished their tests, and Bunk 6 clambered out of the water.

"Did we pass?" pressed Donna, anxious to know the results.

"Hold on a second, Donna. First, I want to tell you I think you have all done well in your swimming classes this year. In fact, Micky, I'm proud of you. For someone afraid of the water, you really conquered your fear."

He paused and looked at his chart where he had checked off the skills they had passed. "Now for the results of your tests. Micky, congratulations. You have made intermediate. Lynn, you are in the swimmer's class. I'm sorry, girls. Unfortunately, the rest of you need work on at least one stroke before I can promote you from intermediate. Better luck next year."

The girls wandered back to the cabin to change for their next period, horseback riding. Micky and Lynn were elated they had passed. While the rest of the girls were disappointed, perhaps they, too, would succeed when they came back to camp next year. It wasn't easy for campers who scarcely knew how to swim at the beginning of the summer to pass their intermediate test as the camp season came to a close.

The rest of the day was uneventful. After riding and lunch, the girls went to their optional activities. Today was their last opportunity to complete all their projects since tomorrow afternoon would be spent preparing for the banquet. Donna glazed the ceramic cup for her father. In Susan's newspaper class, they finished printing this year's final edition.

At dinner, conversation about the banquet practically dominated the entire camp's conversation. Every year, right before the camp season ended, Camp Floridian held a special feast in the mess hall. Everyone wore their best clothes, and an air of frivolity prevailed. Amidst the speeches, counselors gave awards for various activities. This particular meal always meant the close of camp was less than two days away.

During Friday afternoon's rest hour, after the entire camp had attended their general activities, staff delivered trunks and duffle bags to every cabin. Campers and counselors planned to start packing Saturday morning. Everyone would spend the entire day on this activity. First, they would collect the clothes and equipment they had lent to other people. Hopefully, they would fill their trunks and duffle bags with their own possessions.

It wasn't unusual for campers to unpack at home and have towels or socks which belonged to someone else. Camp laundries always managed to lose plenty of additional socks, shorts, and other apparel. What was exceptional, however, was when campers brought home more clothing than they had taken to camp. This was always a surprise to mothers.

Throughout the summer, some campers collected rocks, perhaps for their mineral collections. Others took home a box of sand from the lake. Understanding counselors rescued mothers by not allowing campers to take home a garter snake or frog. Campers brought home other prized possessions such as camp newspapers, a prom favor, their swimming cards, trophies, and the camp play program.

After rest hour, several counselors arranged the tables in the mess hall into an "S" shape, spreading clean white tablecloths over them. They placed flower arrangements in the center of each table to give them a more festive air. Finally, they set up a head table and a speaker's platform for Mrs. Warren, Mike, and the camp directors.

On the boys' side of camp, counselors persuaded their campers, especially the younger boys, to take showers and to wear suits again. On the girls' side, bedlam prevailed. The older girls ran about in robes trying to borrow curling irons, pierced earrings, and other accessories. They ran in and out of cabins until they had either found what they needed or been unsuccessful in their efforts. Usually, they accomplished their goals.

In Bunk 6, the girls also dressed for the banquet. "Susan," asked Janie, as she dressed, "do you think the girls in the senior division are crazy for rushing around like that?"

"Not really, Janie. They want to look especially nice tonight. Remember, the banquet is the season's biggest event. You'll be acting like them when you're their age, maybe even before," reminded Susan.

Janie shook her head vigorously. "Never," she insisted.

Susan laughed to herself as she thought, "What a difference a few years makes. When girls are from eight to ten years of age, they like games and are becoming interested in clothes. However, by the time they reach eleven, hairdos and fashions have to be just right. Janie, too, will learn this eventually. Probably sooner than she thinks."

No dinner whistle blew tonight. Nevertheless, at 6:00 p.m., campers and counselors hustled toward the mess hall. They presented an attractive sight: the girls attired in dresses or pant suits, proud of their hairstyles on which they had worked throughout the afternoon, and the boys in suits or sport jackets. As they entered the mess hall, they went through a receiving line consisting of Mrs. Warren, Mitzi, Mike, and Ted.

The mess hall's interior did not look like a camp building. Instead, it had the appearance of a formal dining hall. Place cards with each camper's or counselor's name were at each table setting. On every plate, lay the final edition of the *Camp Floridian Journal* and a small green card listing the menu and program for the evening.

After everyone sat, they started dining. At all previous meals, huge platters and family sized bowls of food prevailed. Tonight they had individual plates of roast chicken with savory herb dressing, creamy mashed potatoes, fresh string beans, and a tossed salad. At the ends of each table, they found relish trays. With dinner enhanced by the banquet atmosphere, the food actually tasted delicious. While the camp ate dessert, cherry pie a la mode, the program started.

Mrs. Warren rose and asked for everyone's attention. "Boys and girls, counselors, I want to welcome you to the fourth annual Camp Floridian banquet. I hope you are enjoying yourselves. This banquet means another year at our camp is almost over. Each year, this particular evening brings back many wonderful memories. Our camp play, *South Pacific*, which you performed so well, was special. Tonight, Gail Harrison, who played Nellie, will sing some songs from the show. I remember our Camp Talent Show. This year, I can honestly say, we had more talented youngsters than ever before. I remember how you campers went to your different activities and learned skills thanks to our qualified counselors." A round of applause followed.

"Most of all, I remember each of you, as individuals, making Camp Floridian a little better than if you hadn't been here. I want to thank all of you for making this summer a successful one." The owner sat and applause seemed to reach each mess hall corner.

Mike rose from the speaker's table. "Thank you, Mrs. Warren. I'm sure everyone here is glad they were at Camp Floridian this summer. We will now present our entertainment. How about singing for us, Gail?"

Whistles and applause filled the air as Gail came forward. Her performance was delightful with both songs well received.

When Gail finished, Mrs. Warren stood up again. "Thank you very much, Gail. I know everyone enjoyed your singing tremendously."

"I want all of you to become serious for a few minutes. I don't think a camp is well run unless it has good counselors. This year we had the finest group of counselors assembled. I want each of them to stand up when I call his or her name. Campers, let's give them the applause they have earned." She announced each counselor's name. When she called out Susan's name, the girls of Bunk 6 cheered loud and long.

At last, it was time for the awards. Mrs. Warren called Mike to the speaker's platform. "Boys and girls," he announced, "I know this is the moment for which you have all been waiting. We will now distribute the awards. I'm calling Jerry Martin, head of our waterfront, to the microphone. Jerry, will you please come forward."

Jerry walked to the mess hall's front. "I'm calling names of those who have passed their swimming tests this summer. When you hear your name, will you please come forward to receive your cards." It seemed as if Jerry called most of the campers at least once. At last, the long procession ended.

Mike took over. "Now for the big awards. Every year we give two trophies in both the junior and senior divisions, one for the boys and one for the girls, to the campers who are the best in swimming, riding, arts and crafts, and athletics. We also have trophies for the best all-around boy and girl in both age divisions. This year we added one trophy for drama regardless of age or sex. Believe me, I'm one of the counselors who found it tough to judge because so many of you excelled in these particular fields.

"I couldn't make a choice in drama between two of the girls," Mike continued. "Therefore, they're both getting a trophy. One, you just heard sing, Gail Harrison. The other was my assistant in coaching the play. I don't think our staging and prompting could have been done without her help. I neglected to call her on stage when cast members took their bows. However, I'm certainly not overlooking her now. Her name is Janie Barnes, our camper assistant director. Will you two please come forward?"

The girls received their trophies amidst thunderous applause. When Janie returned to the table where her bunkmates sat, the girls admired her trophy, oohing and aahing over it. Janie felt a warm tingle inside as a few tears of happiness fell from her eyes. "At last," she thought, "I've been awarded a trophy that my brother Don can't win."

Her bunkmates were so busy admiring Janie's trophy that when Jean announced the last trophy winner, the girls of Bunk 6 did not hear her. "Ann, are you here?" she called out again.

Ann realized she had won the arts and crafts trophy for the girls' junior division. She gave out a little gasp of joy and limped to the platform. This ended the banquet for the summer. The campers returned to their cabins, reviewing the evening's activities and discussing winners.

Counselors couldn't leave their cabins during the last two nights. Thus, Susan did not have an opportunity to go to the lodge and spend time with Jerry. She admitted this evening had been fun. It had been exciting to wear a dress and heels instead of the usual camp clothes of a T-shirt and jeans.

Ann and Janie remained thrilled about their trophies as they prepared for bed. Janie had also received the red ribbon for coming in second in the Robin Hood Tournament for her age group. None of the girls in Bunk 6 had been awarded the outstanding camper award for junior girls. But trophies won, regardless of the reason, were priceless to winners.

The next day, Saturday, campers and counselors busily packed. Susan assisted her charges whenever they needed help. "Listen, girls," Susan reminded them, "I want you to check for a name tag before you pack any clothing to make sure it's yours. If something doesn't belong to you, please return it immediately."

"And," she continued, "if you lent anything to anyone else in camp, claim it now. I want you to take home all of your own clothing and none of anyone else's."

"Aw, Susan," her girls protested.

It was infallible that mothers would find name tags on articles that didn't belong to their children. It happened every year.

The girls continued to pack. By the afternoon, they had almost finished. After lunch, Mrs. Warren sent for Susan to come to her office. When the counselor arrived, Mrs. Warren motioned for her to sit. Susan settled into the rocker, opposite the camp owner, and prepared to pay attention. She wondered why she had been called.

"Susan," Mrs. Warren began, "I've been very impressed with your work as counselor of Bunk 6. You did a fine job of teaching campers how to produce the *Camp Floridian Journal*. You are also an excellent general counselor. Since we always have a need for your type of staff member, would you consider returning next year as a general counselor? You don't have to give me a definite answer now."

Susan thought for about two seconds. "Mrs. Warren, I'm glad to be associated with Camp Floridian," she exclaimed. "I would love to come back next year."

The camp owner smiled. "That's wonderful. You're an exceptionally good counselor; the type needed in camps, understanding and gentle with campers. I'll look forward to having you here next season."

Susan returned to her cabin feeling satisfied and warm inside. Mrs. Warren had offered her the type of job she enjoyed. Her fondness of children showed in her work.

Just before a late dinner, they finally completed packing. It seemed as if the trunks could not hold any more keepsakes. In addition to containing clothes, they also held a large number of treasures which, in the years to come, would provide their owners with many priceless memories.

Campers and counselors had mixed emotions; therefore, very few conversations took place at the mess hall during dinner. While they looked forward to seeing their families, it was difficult to leave their friends of the past eight weeks. Many campers stared at their food or picked indifferently. They weren't hungry. Emotions were too keen.

At last, all were excused. They wandered to the area where Camp Floridian held a last campfire. Campers and counselors sat around in a circle with their friends. They gazed straight ahead at the huge bonfire with its majestic flames while softly singing camp songs. Susan and Jerry, wanting a final opportunity to be alone, briefly ambled over to the lake by themselves.

"Susan," murmured Jerry, holding her hand as they looked toward the dark water, shining in the moonlight.

"Yes, Jerry," she responded softly.

He bent down and kissed her tenderly then put his arm around her. "You're wonderful," he continued. "It's because of you that I've enjoyed this summer. I want to see you as soon as we get back to Miami. May I?"

"Oh, Jerry, yes," she whispered, nestling her head against his shoulder.

"I wish we could spend some time with each other tomorrow. But, I guess we can't," he complained, "since you'll be boarding the bus early in the morning to take campers home. I have to stay on to Tuesday."

After a moment, he brightened. "I have a great idea," he added. "Let's go out for dinner next weekend."

"I'd love it," Susan replied.

"Fine. I'll call you on Wednesday, and we'll make it definite."

The two counselors embraced before returning to the campfire as the program ended. After the entire camp sang the "Alma Mater" and the "Friendship Song" for the last time that summer, everyone wandered back to their cabins for a final night's rest at camp.

"Just think, girls, tomorrow night you'll be sleeping in your own beds," pointed out Susan as Bunk 6 arrived at the cabin.

"I don't want to go home." Donna was mournful. "I love camp. I hope my parents will send me here next year."

"I hope mine will, too," said Lynn. "Wouldn't it be great if we all came back and camped in the same cabin together?"

"Yes, it would be fabulous," commented Micky. "I want Susan as our counselor, no one else."

Susan smiled at them fondly and reflected on how they seemed to be one happy family. Some problems had been solved. Lynn and Micky were good friends. They no longer vied for bunk leadership but acted as co-leaders. Janie was not as shy as she had been at the beginning of the summer. She joined the others in their activities without being coaxed. Donna had not been homesick after the first week except for a few hours on Visitors Day. This, however, had not been much of a problem, and Donna now had increased confidence about being away from home. Ann had been a delight to have in the group except for her escapade in the woods.

As she prepared for bed, she thought, "This has been a good summer."

The trunks were packed and locked. Tomorrow morning, campers and counselors would strip their beds and place their linens in their duffle bags before they wandered over to the mess hall. After breakfast, they would board buses, leaving behind the lake and fields, trees and cabins. In their place would be memories of the wonderful summer at Camp Floridian.

During camp's last morning, mixed feelings again ran through the entire group. The anticipation of seeing their parents grew greater. So did the sadness in departing Camp Floridian and leaving their bunkmates. There was a flurry of exchanging addresses as all the trunks and duffle bags were being loaded onto the buses. The campers slowly boarded.

At last, with all seated, buses started to move slowly forward. As they passed through the camp gate and headed for the Leesburg train station, they all turned around for a final look at the home they were leaving. Tears fell from many faces.

Some counselors started singing camp songs with others soon joining them. However, most campers sat staring out the windows as they quietly scanned the passing scenery. There were lumps in their throats.

A summer of camp can easily be a rewarding experience for youngsters, and this summer at Camp Floridian had been eight weeks full of fun blended with growth and a few disappointments. Next year, a new season would start. Campers and counselors would enjoy the good times of camping once more.